THE
appetizer
COLLECTION

TRANSCONTINENTAL BOOKS
5800 Saint-Denis St.
Suite 900
Montreal, Que. H2S 3L5
Telephone: 514-273-1066
Toll-free: 1-800-565-5531
canadianliving.com

Bibliothèque et Archives nationales du
Québec and Library and Archives Canada
cataloguing in publication

Main entry under title:
The appetizer collection
"Canadian living".
Includes index.
ISBN 978-0-9877474-4-0
1. Appetizers. 2. Cookbooks. I. Canadian
Living Test Kitchen. II. Canadian living.
III. Title.

TX740.A66 2013   641.81'2
C2013-940271-3

Project editor: Tina Anson Mine
Copy editor: Julia Armstrong
Indexer: Beth Zabloski
Art director and designer: Chris Bond

Printed in Canada
© Transcontinental Books, 2013
Legal deposit – 2nd quarter 2013
National Library of Quebec
National Library of Canada
ISBN 978-0-9877474-4-0

We acknowledge the financial support of
our publishing activity by the Government
of Canada through the Canada Book Fund.

For information on special rates for
corporate libraries and wholesale
purchases, please call 1-866-800-2500.

Canadian Living

THE
appetizer
COLLECTION

BY THE CANADIAN LIVING TEST KITCHEN

Transcontinental Books

EDITOR'S
letter

EVERY YEAR there are a few recipes created in The Test Kitchen that stand out as staff favourites. This past year, the universal winner was Irene Fong's recipe for **Shrimp Sliders With Wasabi Lime Mayo (page 158).** This little burger (pictured above) has everything you could want in a morsel of food: It's a little salty, a little creamy, a little spicy, a little crispy – and utterly delicious. These sliders have made an appearance at every party I've thrown since, and have received rave reviews.

There's something about appetizers that gives them extra appeal. With their abundant flavours and diverse textures, they excite the palate and tease the senses. And since they're so small, you can eat a variety of different types instead of committing to a single dish. That's why, when I throw a party, I almost always choose assorted nibbles over a sit-down dinner. There may be more components to make, but the job is easier because I don't have to plan a meal around a strict set of dietary concerns, likes and dislikes. With the right assortment of hors d'oeuvres, it's guaranteed that there will be something every guest will enjoy.

In this collection, you'll find *Canadian Living*'s best recipes for every type of appetizer. With a wide array of cool dips, savoury sandwiches, flaky handheld pastries, crispy bites and even refreshing cocktails, we have you covered for any type of celebration.

Eat well!

– Annabelle Waugh, director, Food

5

contents

CHAPTER 1

PLAN THE PERFECT
appetizer party

STOCK UP ON SUPPLIES

Not sure how many of everything you'll need? Just do the math.

GLASSES

At least two per person so that each guest can trade in a used one for a clean one at least once. Even if you're serving sparkling wine, simple wineglasses or bistro glasses will do.

PLATES

About three appetizer-size plates per person.

NAPKINS

About three cocktail napkins per person.

ICE

About 8 oz (225 g) per person for a party that's two hours or shorter; about 1 lb (450 g) per person for a party that's three hours or longer.

Prep the Bar

APERITIFS

- Stock up on red and white vermouth, and Campari or Aperol for bitter cocktails. Add some crème de cassis or Grand Marnier for champagne cocktails.

SPIRITS

- The basics are easy: vodka, gin, rum and at least one whiskey, rye, bourbon or scotch.
- If you're not up for mixing cocktails to order, make a signature pitcher cocktail or punch.

NONALCOHOLIC OPTIONS

- Have an array of mixers to make cocktails: tonic water, soda water, ginger ale and cola. For variety, add some juices to the mix and have plenty of citrus fruits to slice and twist.
- A not-too-sweet virgin punch is refreshing. Offer rum, vodka or gin on the side for people who want to spike their drinks.
- Still and sparkling mineral water, as well as pop, are always appreciated.

- Tomato or Clamato are also good options, especially for daytime or summer parties.

WINES

- You don't need to have a huge range – plan on half a bottle per guest.
- Include a dry red, such as Pinot Noir or Cabernet Sauvignon, and a dry white, such as Chardonnay, Sauvignon Blanc or dry Riesling. For variety, offer a semi-dry white, such as Riesling or Vouvray.
- Champagne is nice but pricey. Try a Canadian sparkling wine, Spanish cava, Italian Prosecco or a French sparkler such as Saumur or Crémant d'Alsace.

AFTER-DINNER DRINKS

- Sweet fortified wines, such as cream sherry, Port or icewine, make nice digestifs.
- At holiday parties, eggnog is not really appropriate to serve with food. Save it for the dessert table.

Roasted Red Pepper
Hummus (page 31)

6 *to* 8

OF HORS D'OEUVRES A GUEST WILL EAT PER HOUR FOR THE FIRST COUPLE OF HOURS

Plan Your Menu

- Before you begin, find out if your guests have any dietary restrictions.

- Plan a variety of hot and cold hors d'oeuvres with different colours, textures, temperatures and spiciness levels.

- Choose a number of make-ahead appetizers and/or some that can be made up to a point and quickly finished at the last minute.

- Serve platters of the same food at one time rather than mixed platters, which can make timing tricky.

- Include crowd-pleasing plates of cheese and crackers, antipasti or deli meat, and vegetables and dip.

- Supplement with no-fuss snacks, such as nuts, olives, and tortilla chips and salsa.

11

ADD IT UP

A few quick calculations and you'll know exactly how much food to serve. Per guest, plan on these amounts for your party.

APPETIZERS
6 to 8 pieces per hour; reduce to 4 pieces per hour if dinner follows

CHEESE
1 to 2 oz (30 to 55 g) of each type

SHRIMP
3 to 5

ANTIPASTI & DELI MEATS
2 to 3 oz (55 to 85 g)

CRACKERS
4 to 6

DIPS
2 to 3 tbsp

NUTS
1 to 2 oz (30 to 55 g)

TEA SANDWICHES
4 to 6 pieces

STAY ON BUDGET

Planning is the key. Having a potluck or saying yes when people offer to help reduces cost and workload. Here are more tips to keep your get-together affordable.

Make shopping lists and keep ingredient prices in mind when planning menu and drink choices.

Bulk up crudité platters with economical vegetables, such as carrots, celery, radishes and green peppers. Use pricey choices, such as red peppers and snow peas, sparingly.

Cheese and nuts are costly; try popcorn and pretzels instead.

Choose meatless appetizers or less-expensive cuts of meat.

Offer economical dips, which stretch a long way.

Set Up the Venue

- Stick to one decorative theme; focus on one or two colours or a suitable motif.

- Think of crowd flow and movement. Position the serving table so that it's accessible from both sides. If you have room, create separate food stations and a bar to prevent people from clustering in one area.

- Create an interesting tabletop landscape by varying the shapes, sizes and heights of platters, bowls and stands.

- Set trays, platters and bowls of goodies on tables to let guests help themselves.

- Stack small dishes and cocktail napkins near platters of food and at both ends of the table.

- Set out small bowls for discarding olive pits, shrimp tails and cocktail picks.

Keep Food Safe

To keep appetizers fresh, appealing and safe to eat, don't let them stand at room temperature for very long – definitely not more than two hours. Arrange each variety on a small platter, then cover and refrigerate. Put out only as many as you need to begin the party and keep an eye on them. When they run out, instead of adding replacements to platters that have been standing at room temperature, bring out a fresh, full platter and pass it around to hungry guests.

Honey Apple Snack Mix
(page 232)

WORK PLAN

Four Weeks Ahead

- ☐ Set budget.
- ☐ Make guest list and send invitations.
- ☐ Plan menu, table settings and decorations.
- ☐ Write checklist, prioritizing preparations.

Two Weeks Ahead

- ☐ Check off pantry staples on hand.
- ☐ Prepare shopping list.
- ☐ Shop for nonperishable goods.
- ☐ Arrange rentals, such as plates, platters and glasses, if necessary.
- ☐ Clean and polish glasses; purchase inexpensive glassware or disposables (preferably recyclable) if you need extras.
- ☐ Prepare whatever make-ahead items you can.

Two Days Ahead

- ☐ Clean your home (save time by worrying about only the rooms guests will see).
- ☐ Clean and clear out refrigerator and freezer to make enough space for food.
- ☐ Shop for perishables.
- ☐ Prepare remaining make-ahead foods.
- ☐ Chill beverages.
- ☐ Fill ice cube trays or purchase bags of ice.
- ☐ Set up serving table(s), complete with plates, napkins, cutlery and glasses.
- ☐ Decorate room(s).
- ☐ Choose and have music ready to go.

Day of Party

- ☐ Complete food and beverage prep.
- ☐ Clear space for guests' coats and bags.

Party Time

- ☐ Complete and plate party food.
- ☐ Set out drinks and ice.
- ☐ Light candles and turn on music.
- ☐ Relax and have fun!

13

dips & spreads

Clockwise from left: Smoked Salmon & Artichoke Dip (page 54), Colourful Vegetarian Pâté (page 27) and Potted Cheddar With Port (page 46)

Herbes de Provence Dip

Simple fridge and pantry staples are the keys to this easy dip, which you can make ahead or whip up at the last minute. Serve with about 1 cup loosely packed vegetable crudités per person.

½ cup **cream cheese,** softened

½ cup **sour cream**

½ cup **light mayonnaise**

½ tsp **Dijon mustard**

½ tsp **herbes de Provence**

¼ tsp each **garlic powder** and **onion powder**

Pinch each **salt** and **pepper**

Dash **hot pepper sauce**

1 tbsp chopped **fresh chives**

In bowl, beat together cream cheese, sour cream, mayonnaise and mustard until smooth.

Beat in herbes de Provence, garlic and onion powders, salt, pepper and hot pepper sauce; stir in chives. *(Make-ahead: Cover and refrigerate for up to 24 hours.)*

Change It Up

RANCH DIP
Substitute 1 tbsp chopped fresh dill (or ¼ tsp dried dillweed) for herbes de Provence.

16

Makes 1½ cups. PER 1 TBSP: about 41 cal, 1 g pro, 4 g total fat (2 g sat. fat), 1 g carb, 0 g fibre, 9 mg chol, 51 mg sodium. % RDI: 1% calcium, 1% iron, 3% vit A, 1% folate.

From left: Herbes de Provence Dip
(opposite) and Smoky Hummus (page 34)

Basil Aïoli

Garden-fresh basil gives this dip great flavour. It's delicious as a summer party starter with crudités, or as a dip for Crispy Calamari (page 76).

⅔ cup lightly packed **fresh basil leaves**

⅓ cup **extra-virgin olive oil**

1 clove **garlic,** minced

1 tbsp **lemon juice**

Dash **hot pepper sauce**

1½ cups **mayonnaise** or light mayonnaise

In food processor, pulse together basil, oil, garlic, lemon juice and hot pepper sauce until smooth; pulse in mayonnaise. *(Make-ahead: Refrigerate in airtight container for up to 24 hours.)*

How-To

BLANCHING CRUDITÉS

Blanching veggies keeps them crisp and intensifies their colour. To go with this aïoli, choose an assortment of vegetables (such as carrots, green beans, peppers and zucchini) and cut enough to make 6 cups sticks. Blanch in boiling water just until colours brighten, about 1 minute. Drain; immediately chill in ice water. Drain well.

18

Makes about 2 cups. PER 1 TBSP: about 94 cal, trace pro, 10 g total fat (2 g sat. fat), 1 g carb, 0 g fibre, 4 mg chol, 59 mg sodium. % RDI: 1% iron, 1% vit A.

Smoky Red Pepper Dip

This dip has a slight spicy kick. You can use a dried ancho or morita chili instead of the chipotle pepper if you wish. To rehydrate it, place in small bowl and cover with boiling water; let stand for 30 minutes, then drain.

2 drained **jarred roasted red peppers**

1 **canned chipotle pepper in adobo sauce**

1 pkg (250 g) **light cream cheese,** softened

½ cup **light sour cream**

1 tsp **sweet paprika**

1 tsp **chili powder**

2 cloves **garlic**

2 tsp grated **lemon zest**

2 tbsp **lemon juice**

2 tbsp minced **fresh cilantro**

1 tbsp minced **fresh chives** or green onion

In food processor, purée roasted red peppers with chipotle pepper, scraping down side of bowl several times.

Add cream cheese, sour cream, paprika and chili powder; purée until blended. Pulse in garlic, lemon zest and juice, cilantro and chives.

Scrape into serving bowl; cover and refrigerate until chilled, about 1 hour. *(Make-ahead: Refrigerate for up to 2 days.)*

19

Makes 2 cups. PER 1 TBSP: about 26 cal, 1 g pro, 2 g total fat (1 g sat. fat), 2 g carb, trace fibre, 7 mg chol, 48 mg sodium. % RDI: 2% calcium, 1% iron, 4% vit A, 23% vit C, 1% folate.

Caponata

This Sicilian sweet-and-sour eggplant relish or salad is often served as part of an antipasto platter. It can also be spooned onto toasted baguette slices or used as a base for pasta sauce.

1 large **eggplant** (about 1½ lb/675 g)

3¼ tsp **salt**

¼ cup **pine nuts**

½ cup **extra-virgin olive oil**

2 ribs **celery,** diced

1 **onion,** diced

1 **sweet red pepper,** diced

1 clove **garlic,** minced

¼ cup **golden raisins**

¼ cup quartered **green olives**

¼ cup **red wine vinegar**

2 tbsp rinsed drained **capers**

1 tbsp **granulated sugar**

¼ tsp **pepper**

2 tbsp chopped **fresh basil** or fresh parsley

Cut eggplant into ½-inch (1 cm) cubes; toss with 1 tbsp of the salt. Transfer to colander; let drain for 30 minutes.

Meanwhile, in dry small skillet, toast pine nuts over medium heat, stirring often, until light golden, about 3 minutes. Set aside.

Rinse eggplant; drain and pat dry. In large nonstick skillet, heat 2 tbsp of the oil over medium-high heat; sauté eggplant, in batches, until golden, about 12 minutes. Transfer to bowl; set aside.

In large saucepan, heat 2 tbsp of the remaining oil over medium heat; fry celery and onion until softened, about 8 minutes. Add red pepper, garlic and remaining salt; cook, stirring, until softened, about 5 minutes.

Stir in raisins, olives, vinegar, capers, sugar and pepper. Stir in eggplant and remaining oil; cover and simmer for 5 minutes. Let cool for 10 minutes. Stir in pine nuts and basil. Serve warm or at room temperature. *(Make-ahead: Let cool completely. Refrigerate in airtight container for up to 1 week; let come to room temperature before serving.)*

21

Makes about 4 cups. PER 1 TBSP: about 27 cal, trace pro, 2 g total fat (1 g sat. fat), 2 g carb, 1 g fibre, 0 mg chol, 27 mg sodium. % RDI: 1% iron, 1% vit A, 6% vit C, 1% folate.

Artichoke & Asiago Cheese Spread

Trendy and incredibly appetizing, this dip is delicious with crisp tortilla chips. Set aside an artichoke heart for garnish.

1 can (14 oz/398 mL) **artichoke hearts,** drained and rinsed

1 cup **sour cream**

¾ cup shredded **Asiago cheese**

2 tbsp chopped **fresh parsley**

1 tbsp **Dijon mustard**

½ tsp grated **lemon zest**

½ tsp each **salt** and **pepper**

Pinch **cayenne pepper**

1 clove **garlic,** minced

¼ cup **fresh bread crumbs**

In food processor, purée together artichokes, sour cream, Asiago cheese, parsley, Dijon mustard, lemon zest, salt, pepper and cayenne pepper until smooth. Stir in garlic.

Scrape into ovenproof 2-cup (500 mL) serving dish. *(Make-ahead: Cover with plastic wrap and refrigerate for up to 2 days. Or overwrap with foil and freeze for up to 2 weeks; bake from frozen, increasing baking time by 20 minutes.)* Sprinkle with bread crumbs.

Bake on rimmed baking sheet in 400°F (200°C) oven until edge is bubbly and bread crumbs are golden, about 20 minutes.

22

Makes 2 cups. PER 1 TBSP: about 26 cal, 1 g pro, 2 g total fat (1 g sat. fat), 2 g carb, trace fibre, 5 mg chol, 96 mg sodium. % RDI: 3% calcium, 1% iron, 2% vit A, 2% vit C, 2% folate.

Smoky Eggplant Dip

Smoked paprika adds an earthy note to this nondairy dip. If you're not a fan of smoke, sweet paprika is delicious, too. Serve with Pita Crisps (page 131), Lavash (page 133) or crudités.

1 head **garlic**

3 tbsp **extra-virgin olive oil**

1 large **eggplant** (about 1¼ lb/565 g)

1 tbsp **sherry vinegar**

1 tsp **smoked paprika**

½ tsp **salt**

⅛ tsp **cayenne pepper**

2 tbsp minced **fresh parsley**

Trim top off garlic to expose cloves. Place on small square of foil and drizzle with ½ tsp of the olive oil; seal to form package and place on foil-lined baking sheet.

With fork, prick eggplant all over; add to pan. Roast in 400°F (200°C) oven until eggplant is very tender when tested with fork and garlic is soft, 50 to 60 minutes. Slit eggplant lengthwise and open. Unwrap garlic; let cool.

Scoop eggplant flesh into food processor or bowl; squeeze in garlic pulp. Purée or mash well with fork. Blend in remaining oil, vinegar, paprika, salt and cayenne pepper; stir in parsley. Scrape into serving bowl; cover and refrigerate for 1 hour. *(Make-ahead: Refrigerate for up to 2 days.)*

23

Makes about 2 cups. PER 1 TBSP: about 19 cal, 1 g pro, 2 g total fat (trace sat. fat), 2 g carb, 1 g fibre, 0 mg chol, 37 mg sodium, 29 mg potassium. % RDI: 1% calcium, 1% iron, 1% vit A, 2% vit C, 2% folate.

Warm Mediterranean Spinach Dip

This lower-fat version of classic creamy spinach dip is best served on slices of crusty Italian bread or baguette, or with flatbreads for dipping.

2 bags (10 oz/284 g each) **fresh spinach,** washed and trimmed

2 tbsp **extra-virgin olive oil**

2 cloves **garlic,** minced

1 **anchovy fillet,** chopped (or 1 tsp anchovy paste)

¾ tsp **fennel seeds**

¼ tsp each **hot pepper flakes** and **salt**

1 bottle (680 mL) **strained tomatoes** (passata)

½ cup grated **Romano cheese** or Parmesan cheese

In batches, place spinach in large pot with just the water clinging to leaves; cover and cook over medium-high heat, stirring once, until wilted, about 3 minutes. Transfer to sieve; press out moisture. Chop and set aside.

In skillet, heat oil over medium heat; cook garlic, anchovy, fennel seeds, hot pepper flakes and salt, stirring constantly, until fragrant and garlic is light golden, about 1 minute.

Stir in tomatoes and spinach; cook until heated through, about 2 minutes. *(Make-ahead: Let cool. Refrigerate in airtight container for up to 2 days.)*

Spread in 9-inch (23 cm) pie plate or shallow baking dish; sprinkle with cheese. Broil until hot and bubbly and cheese is golden, about 3 minutes.

24

Makes 4 cups. PER 1 TBSP: about 13 cal, 1 g pro, 1 g total fat (0 g sat. fat), 2 g carb, 1 g fibre, 1 mg chol, 30 mg sodium, 88 mg potassium. % RDI: 2% calcium, 4% iron, 9% vit A, 4% vit C, 6% folate.

Creamy Herb Dip

Served with either chips or vegetables, this quick and easy dip (and its equally delicious variations) won't last long. Try an assortment of flavours for an open house or holiday party.

½ cup **sour cream**

½ cup **cream cheese,** softened

½ cup **mayonnaise**

Pinch each **salt** and **pepper**

SEASONINGS:

¼ tsp each **dried oregano** and **dried thyme**

¼ tsp each **garlic powder** and **onion powder**

In food processor, purée together sour cream, cream cheese, mayonnaise, salt and pepper until smooth.

SEASONINGS: Add oregano, thyme, garlic powder and onion powder; pulse to combine, scraping down side of bowl as necessary.

26

Change It Up

CREAMY CURRY DIP
Omit salt, pepper and Seasonings. Substitute 1 tbsp mild curry paste and ¼ tsp ground turmeric.

CREAMY RED PEPPER DIP
Omit Seasonings. Substitute 2 jarred roasted red peppers, drained and patted dry; 1 clove garlic, minced; and ½ tsp dried basil.

CREAMY CARAMELIZED ONION DIP
Omit salt, pepper and Seasonings. In large saucepan, heat 2 tbsp vegetable oil over medium-low heat; cook 1 Spanish onion, thinly sliced; ½ tsp dried thyme; and pinch each salt and pepper until onion is tender and golden, about 30 minutes. Add to sour cream mixture along with 1 tsp red wine vinegar; pulse until combined.

CREAMY AVOCADO DIP
Omit Seasonings. Substitute 1 avocado, pitted, peeled and chopped; 1 green onion, sliced; and 1 tbsp lime juice.

Makes 1½ cups. PER 1 TBSP: about 57 cal, 1 g pro, 6 g total fat (2 g sat. fat), 1 g carb, 0 g fibre, 9 mg chol, 42 mg sodium. % RDI: 1% calcium, 1% iron, 3% vit A, 1% folate.

Colourful Vegetarian Pâté

Pretty layers of colour and fresh flavours make this so-simple pâté a winner. The best part? You can make it up to two days ahead. Garnish with fresh basil and serve with toasted baguette slices, melba toasts or crackers.

1 can (19 oz/540 mL) **white kidney beans,** drained and rinsed

1 tsp **lemon juice**

¼ cup **olive oil**

¼ tsp each **ground cumin** and **pepper**

1 pkg (250 g) **light cream cheese,** softened

¾ cup chopped drained jarred **roasted red peppers**

2 cups lightly packed **fresh basil leaves**

¼ cup **pine nuts**

2 cloves **garlic,** minced

½ cup grated **Parmesan cheese**

In food processor, purée kidney beans. Add lemon juice, 1 tsp of the oil, cumin and pepper; process until smooth. Spoon into plastic wrap–lined 8- x 4-inch (1.5 L) loaf pan; cover and refrigerate.

In food processor, purée cream cheese with red pepper until smooth. Spread over bean layer; cover and refrigerate.

In food processor, combine basil, pine nuts and garlic. With machine running, gradually add remaining oil and process until coarse paste forms. Pulse in Parmesan cheese. Spread over red pepper layer. Cover and refrigerate until set, about 8 hours. *(Make-ahead: Refrigerate for up to 2 days.)*

Invert onto serving platter; remove plastic wrap.

27

Makes 16 servings. PER SERVING: about 127 cal, 5 g pro, 9 g total fat (3 g sat. fat), 7 g carb, 3 g fibre, 16 mg chol, 207 mg sodium. % RDI: 7% calcium, 4% iron, 4% vit A, 18% vit C, 9% folate.

Spiced Lentil Topping (opposite)
and Pita Crisps (page 131)

Spiced Lentil Topping

This warm curry-scented dip is especially good served on Pita Crisps (page 131). Garnish with fresh cilantro sprigs for a touch of colour.

1 tbsp **extra-virgin olive oil**

Half **onion,** finely chopped

1 small clove **garlic,** minced

1 tsp grated **fresh ginger**
    (or ¼ tsp ground ginger)

½ tsp **ground turmeric**

½ tsp **ground cumin**

Pinch each **salt** and
    cayenne pepper

1 cup **dried red lentils**

Half can (28 oz/796 mL can)
    diced tomatoes

1½ tsp **lemon juice**

2 tbsp chopped **fresh cilantro**
    or fresh parsley

In saucepan, heat oil over medium heat; fry onion, garlic, ginger, turmeric, cumin, salt and cayenne pepper, stirring often, until onion is softened, about 5 minutes.

Stir in lentils and tomatoes; bring to boil. Reduce heat, cover and simmer, stirring often, until lentils are softened but still hold their shape, about 20 minutes. Stir in lemon juice; let cool slightly. *(Make-ahead: Refrigerate in airtight container for up to 2 days. Reheat to serve.)*

Stir in cilantro just before serving.

29

Makes 2 cups. PER 1 TBSP: about 28 cal, 2 g pro, 1 g total fat (0 g sat. fat), 4 g carb, 1 g fibre, 0 mg chol, 19 mg sodium. % RDI: 1% calcium, 5% iron, 1% vit A, 3% vit C, 15% folate.

Broccoli & Cheddar White Bean Spread

Broccoli isn't usually on the list when you think of party food, but here it's a fresh, green addition to a classic cheese-laced bean dip.

1½ cups **broccoli florets**

1 can (19 oz/540 mL) **cannellini beans** or white kidney beans, drained and rinsed

1 cup shredded **old Cheddar cheese**

1 clove **garlic,** minced

3 tbsp **olive oil**

3 tbsp **lemon juice**

¼ tsp each **salt** and **pepper**

In saucepan of boiling salted water, cover and cook broccoli until tender-crisp, about 2 minutes. Drain and chill in cold water; drain well. Transfer to food processor.

Add beans, Cheddar cheese, garlic, oil, lemon juice, salt and pepper; purée until smooth.

How-To

TOASTING PITA WEDGES

Toasted pita wedges are tasty, easy-to-make partners for dips. For a heartier texture and flavour, try whole-grain Greek pitas. Cut them into wedges, then toast or broil for a minute or two (a toaster oven works perfectly). The edges should be crisp and the centres still nice and tender.

30

Makes 2½ cups. PER 1 TBSP: about 31 cal, 1 g pro, 2 g total fat (1 g sat. fat), 2 g carb, 1 g fibre, 3 mg chol, 68 mg sodium, 37 mg potassium. % RDI: 2% calcium, 1% iron, 2% vit A, 3% vit C, 3% folate.

Roasted Red Pepper Hummus

Why buy this party staple at the grocery store when it's a cinch to make fresh at home? The recipe is easily doubled for a crowd.

1 can (19 oz/540 mL) **chickpeas,** drained and rinsed

½ cup chopped drained **jarred roasted red peppers**

¼ cup **lemon juice**

¼ cup **tahini**

¼ cup **extra-virgin olive oil**

¼ tsp each **salt** and **pepper**

2 cloves **garlic,** minced

In food processor, purée chickpeas with red peppers until smooth.

Add lemon juice, tahini, oil, salt and pepper; blend until creamy, adding a little water to thin, if desired. Stir in garlic.

Change It Up

SESAME ROASTED RED PEPPER HUMMUS

If you don't have any tahini on hand, substitute 1 tbsp sesame oil. Thin down the hummus with a bit of water if it's too thick for your liking.

31

Makes about 2 cups. PER 1 TBSP: about 38 cal, trace pro, 2 g total fat (trace sat. fat), 4 g carb, 1 g fibre, 0 mg chol, 65 mg sodium. % RDI: 1% calcium, 1% iron, 1% vit A, 10% vit C, 4% folate.

Country Pâté

The flavours of this highly seasoned pâté mellow as it cures. If you like crisp bacon, brown the whole loaf of pâté in a skillet over medium heat, 1 minute per side. Serve with Dijon mustard, baguette slices and cornichons.

1 tsp **black peppercorns** or ground pepper

10 **allspice berries** (or 1 tsp ground allspice)

3 **whole cloves** (or pinch ground cloves)

1 lb (450 g) **lean ground pork**

8 oz (225 g) **ground veal**

½ cup **unsalted shelled pistachios**

¼ cup finely chopped **shallots**

3 tbsp **cognac** or brandy

1 tbsp **cornstarch**

2½ tsp **coarse sea salt**

2 tsp chopped **fresh thyme**

1 clove **garlic,** minced

1 lb (450 g) **bacon**

4 oz (115 g) piece **Black Forest ham,** cut in thick strips

CHICKEN MIXTURE:

8 oz (225 g) **boneless skinless chicken thighs,** halved lengthwise

6 oz (170 g) **chicken livers,** trimmed and chopped

1 tbsp **cognac** or brandy

½ tsp **salt**

¼ tsp **pepper**

In spice grinder, finely grind peppercorns, allspice and cloves if using whole (or, in bowl, mix ground spices). Combine spices, pork, veal, pistachios, shallots, cognac, cornstarch, salt, thyme and garlic. Cover with plastic wrap; refrigerate for 3 hours. *(Make-ahead: Refrigerate for up to 24 hours.)*

CHICKEN MIXTURE: Meanwhile, combine chicken thighs and livers, cognac, salt and pepper. Cover with plastic wrap; refrigerate for 3 hours. *(Make-ahead: Refrigerate for up to 24 hours.)*

Line terrine mould or 8- x 4-inch (1.5 L) loaf pan with bacon, leaving enough overhang to cover top. Gently press one-third of the pork mixture into mould. Arrange chicken thighs lengthwise in mould. Press half of the remaining pork mixture over top. Arrange livers in row down centre. Arrange ham along either side of livers. Gently press remaining pork mixture over top; smooth top. Fold bacon overhang up to cover completely.

Place mould on large double-thickness square of foil; bring sides up and over to cover, folding seam in centre several times to seal. Place in roasting pan; pour in enough warm water to come halfway up sides of mould. Bake in 325°F (160°C) oven until instant-read thermometer inserted into centre reads 170°F (77°C), 2½ hours. Unwrap mould; let cool for 30 minutes. Refrigerate until cold, 3 hours. Wrap in plastic wrap; refrigerate for 24 hours. *(Make-ahead: Refrigerate for up to 4 days.)*

Run knife around mould; invert pâté onto cutting board. Scrape away gelatin. Slice with hot knife.

Makes 10 servings. PER SERVING: about 421 cal, 28 g pro, 31 g total fat (15 g sat. fat), 5 g carb, 1 g fibre, 175 mg chol, 994 mg sodium, 498 mg potassium. % RDI: 2% calcium, 22% iron, 86% vit A, 10% vit C, 45% folate.

Smoky Hummus

This dip has a tangy zip from the yogurt and lemon juice, and a hint of delicious smokiness from the paprika. Leftovers are nice on sandwiches, so plan on making a double batch of the hummus.

1 can (19 oz/540 mL) **chickpeas,** drained and rinsed

½ cup **Balkan-style plain yogurt**

3 tbsp **extra-virgin olive oil**

1 tsp grated **lemon zest**

4 tsp **lemon juice**

¼ tsp **salt**

1 clove **garlic,** minced

¼ tsp **smoked paprika**

In food processor, purée together chickpeas, yogurt, oil, lemon zest, lemon juice, salt and garlic until smooth.

Add smoked paprika; pulse until combined. *(Make-ahead: Refrigerate in airtight container for up to 2 days.)*

34

How-To

GETTING THE GARLIC SMELL OFF YOUR FINGERS

The aroma of garlic really can linger on your hands. After chopping garlic, rinse your hands under running water while rubbing your fingers against something made from stainless steel. Kitchenware stores often sell pieces of stainless steel in the shape of a bar of soap for this purpose, but the side of a knife (watch the sharp edge!) will do just as nicely.

Makes 1¾ cups. PER 1 TBSP: about 37 cal, 1 g pro, 2 g total fat (trace sat. fat), 4 g carb, 1 g fibre, 1 mg chol, 65 mg sodium, 35 mg potassium. % RDI: 1% calcium, 1% iron, 2% vit C, 4% folate.

White Bean & Rosemary Dip

Fresh rosemary tastes less woody than dried. Here, it gives a pleasant, grassy note to a delicate bean dip.

1 can (19 oz/540 mL) **white kidney beans,** drained and rinsed

2 tbsp chopped **fresh rosemary**

2 tbsp **lemon juice**

1 tbsp **extra-virgin olive oil**

¼ tsp **salt**

2 cloves **garlic,** minced

1 tbsp **red pepper jelly**

In food processor, purée together beans, rosemary, lemon juice, 2 tbsp water, oil and salt until smooth; stir in garlic.

Scrape into serving bowl. *(Make-ahead: Cover and refrigerate for up to 2 days.)* Spoon jelly onto centre of dip.

35

Change It Up

WHITE BEAN & THYME DIP

Substitute fresh thyme for the rosemary, and olive tapenade or sun-dried tomato pesto for the red pepper jelly.

Makes 1⅔ cups. PER 1 TBSP: about 22 cal, 1 g pro, 1 g total fat (0 g sat. fat), 3 g carb, 1 g fibre, 0 mg chol, 73 mg sodium. % RDI: 1% iron, 2% vit C, 4% folate.

Chicken Liver Mousse

Clarified butter not only seals the mousse in little pots (helping to extend shelf life) but also adds another layer of luxuriousness to this creamy spread. Let it chill for at least 24 hours to allow the flavours to develop.

8 oz (225 g) **chicken livers**

½ tsp each **salt** and **pepper**

½ cup **unsalted butter**

½ cup chopped **shallots**

⅓ cup thinly sliced peeled **Granny Smith apple**

1 clove **garlic,** finely chopped

1 tsp finely chopped **fresh thyme**

3 tbsp **sherry** or brandy

1 tsp finely chopped **fresh chives**

Separate lobes of livers, removing any connective tissue and fat; sprinkle with half each of the salt and pepper.

In skillet, melt 1 tbsp of the butter over medium heat; cook shallots, apple, garlic and thyme, stirring often, until softened, about 5 minutes. Push to side of pan.

Melt 2 tsp of the remaining butter in same pan over medium-high heat; cook livers, turning once, until just a hint of pink remains in centre of thickest part, about 3 minutes. Add sherry; cook for 30 seconds.

Scrape into food processor; purée until smooth. Let cool slightly in processor. Cut ¼ cup of the remaining butter into pieces. With food processor running, drop in butter, piece by piece and waiting until combined before adding next piece. Sprinkle in remaining salt and pepper; purée until shiny, about 1 minute.

Using large spoon, press through fine sieve into bowl. Scrape into two ¾-cup (175 mL) ramekins or dishes. Cover with plastic wrap; refrigerate until set, about 1 hour. Uncover; sprinkle with chives.

In small saucepan or microwaveable glass measure, melt remaining butter; skim froth from surface. Pour over chives, leaving any milky sediment behind. Re-cover and chill until mousse is set, about 24 hours. *(Make-ahead: Cover with plastic wrap and refrigerate for up to 4 days.)*

37

Makes about 1 cup. PER 1 TBSP: about 78 cal, 3 g pro, 6 g total fat (4 g sat. fat), 2 g carb, trace fibre, 77 mg chol, 84 mg sodium, 57 mg potassium. % RDI: 1% calcium, 9% iron, 76% vit A, 7% vit C, 34% folate.

Potted Camembert

Make-ahead appetizers that wait patiently in the fridge make party planning easy. Whip up this rich cheese a day or two in advance and garnish just before serving.

2 cups cubed **Camembert cheese** (about 10 oz/280 g), softened

Half pkg (250 g pkg) **light cream cheese,** softened

⅓ cup **light sour cream**

3 tbsp chopped **shallots** or white part of green onions

½ tsp **pepper**

¼ cup finely chopped **fresh chives** or green part of green onions

In food processor, purée together Camembert cheese, cream cheese, sour cream, shallots and pepper until smooth.

Scrape cheese mixture into serving bowl; stir in all but 1 tsp of the chives. *(Make-ahead: Cover and refrigerate for up to 2 days.)*

Garnish with remaining chives.

38

Change It Up

POTTED BRIE
Substitute Brie cheese for the Camembert.

POTTED CAMBOZOLA
Substitute Cambozola cheese for the Camembert.

Makes 2 cups. PER 1 TBSP: about 39 cal, 2 g pro, 3 g total fat (2 g sat. fat), 1 g carb, 0 g fibre, 9 mg chol, 104 mg sodium. % RDI: 4% calcium, 1% iron, 3% vit A, 3% folate.

Blue Cheese Dip

Calling all blue cheese lovers! This dip can be strong or mild, depending on the type of cheese you use. It's particularly nice if you splurge on Roquefort or Stilton, but Danish blue is a tasty, economical choice.

½ cup **light mayonnaise**

¼ cup **light sour cream**

1 tbsp chopped **fresh dill**
   (or ¼ tsp dried dillweed)

1 tsp **wine vinegar**

1 clove **garlic,** minced

¼ tsp **hot pepper sauce**

Pinch **pepper**

⅓ cup crumbled **blue cheese**

In bowl, stir together mayonnaise, sour cream, dill, vinegar, garlic, hot pepper sauce and pepper.

Stir in blue cheese. (*Make-ahead: Cover and refrigerate for up to 2 days.*)

Change It Up

GOAT CHEESE OR FETA DIP

If you're not a fan of blue cheese, this base works just as well with goat cheese or feta cheese.

39

Makes about ¾ cup. PER 1 TBSP: about 50 cal, 1 g pro, 4 g total fat (1 g sat. fat), 2 g carb, 0 g fibre, 7 mg chol, 130 mg sodium. % RDI: 3% calcium, 1% vit A.

Classic Cheese Ball

Though you could use another type of Cheddar, the extra-old orange-coloured variety provides the ultimate in flavour and appearance.

½ cup toasted chopped **pecans** or walnuts

CHEESE BALL BASE:

2 cups shredded **extra-old Cheddar cheese** (about 8 oz/225 g)

1 pkg (250 g) **cream cheese,** softened

2 tbsp **tawny Port,** white Port, bourbon, whiskey or whipping cream (35%)

1 tsp **dry mustard**

¼ tsp **cayenne pepper**

CHEESE BALL BASE: In food processor, purée together Cheddar cheese, cream cheese, Port, mustard and cayenne pepper until smooth. Scrape into plastic wrap–lined bowl; cover and refrigerate until firm but still pliable, about 30 minutes. *(Make-ahead: Refrigerate for up to 5 days or overwrap and freeze for up to 1 month.)*

Place pecans in shallow bowl; peel plastic wrap off cheese. Using hands, mould cheese into ball. Roll in nuts, pressing to coat all over. Wrap and refrigerate until firm, about 2 hours.

Change It Up

GRAPE & CHEESE BALL TRUFFLES

Make Cheese Ball Base; refrigerate until firm yet pliable, 30 minutes. For each truffle, scoop about 1 tbsp of base; mould around 1 seedless grape to enclose. Combine 1 cup finely chopped toasted pecans or walnuts, and 1 tbsp chopped fresh parsley (optional), on plate; roll truffles in mixture to coat. Cover and refrigerate on waxed paper–lined tray until firm, 2 hours. **Makes about 32 pieces.**

CHEESE BALL SNOWMAN

Make Cheese Ball Base using white Cheddar cheese; refrigerate until firm yet pliable, about 30 minutes. Divide into 3 slightly different-size balls; roll in ⅓ cup grated Parmesan or Romano cheese. On plate, stack balls to make snowman; decorate with peppercorns or currants for eyes and buttons, roasted red pepper strip for mouth and baby carrot for nose. Refrigerate until firm, about 2 hours. **Makes about 2 cups.**

CURRY MANGO CHEESE SPREAD

Make Cheese Ball Base, omitting Port. Stir in ¼ cup mango chutney (chop solids if large) and 1 tsp curry paste. Line 9-inch (23 cm) pie plate with plastic wrap; sprinkle with ½ cup chopped roasted cashews. Spread cheese mixture over top; cover and refrigerate until firm, about 2 hours. Invert onto plate. **Makes about 2 cups.**

Makes about 2 cups. PER 1 TBSP: about 69 cal, 3 g pro, 6 g total fat (3 g sat. fat), 1 g carb, trace fibre, 16 mg chol, 67 mg sodium, 25 mg potassium. % RDI: 5% calcium, 1% iron, 5% vit A, 1% folate.

Grape & Cheese Ball
Truffles (opposite)

Goat Cheese Roasted Red Pepper Dip

Yogurt and goat cheese give this dip a tangy edge that balances the sweetness of the red peppers. Garnish with chopped fresh parsley, chopped fresh chives or rosemary sprigs.

8 oz (225 g) **soft goat cheese**

¾ cup chopped drained **jarred roasted red peppers**

½ cup **plain yogurt**

2 tbsp **olive oil**

1 clove **garlic,** minced

½ tsp each crumbled **dried rosemary** and crushed **fennel seeds**

¼ tsp each **salt** and **pepper**

2 tbsp chopped **fresh parsley**

2 tbsp chopped **fresh chives** or green onions

In food processor, purée together goat cheese, red peppers, yogurt, olive oil, garlic, rosemary, fennel seeds, salt and pepper.

Pulse in parsley and chives. Transfer to serving bowl; smooth top. *(Make-ahead: Cover and refrigerate for up to 2 days.)*

42

How-To

ROASTING RED PEPPERS

Jarred roasted red peppers are perfectly fine, but freshly roasted peppers are the ultimate in flavour and texture. To make them, place sweet red peppers on greased grill over medium heat; cover and grill, turning often, until charred, 10 to 12 minutes. (Or arrange peppers on baking sheet; broil, turning often, until charred, about 15 minutes.) Place peppers in bowl; cover with plastic wrap and let cool. Peel off skin and seed peppers.

Makes about 2 cups. PER 1 TBSP: about 31 cal, 2 g pro, 3 g total fat (1 g sat. fat), 1 g carb, trace fibre, 4 mg chol, 47 mg sodium. % RDI: 2% calcium, 2% iron, 5% vit A, 10% vit C, 1% folate.

Warm Blue Cheese & Leek Spread

This rich, sophisticated and warm spin on onion dip is a heavenly way to start an evening. Leeks can be hard to clean, but our handy how-to (below) makes it simple to get the grit out.

3 **leeks** (white and light green parts only)

1 pkg (250 g) **cream cheese,** softened

½ cup **sour cream**

¼ tsp each **salt** and **pepper**

⅛ tsp **nutmeg**

1½ cups crumbled **blue cheese** (about 6 oz/170 g)

3 tbsp toasted **sliced almonds**

Trim leeks and halve lengthwise. In saucepan of simmering salted water, cover and poach leeks until tender, about 10 minutes. Drain and let cool. Press out liquid; finely chop. Set aside.

In food processor, purée together cream cheese, sour cream, salt, pepper and nutmeg; transfer to bowl. Stir in leeks and blue cheese; spread in 9-inch (23 cm) pie plate or shallow baking dish. *(Make-ahead: Cover and refrigerate for up to 2 days.)*

Bake in 400°F (200°C) oven until golden, hot and bubbly, about 30 minutes. Sprinkle with almonds.

43

How-To

CLEANING LEEKS

Cut off dark green tops. Leaving base intact, cut off roots, then, beginning just above base, slit in half lengthwise. Hold, base up, under running water and separate layers. If you need chopped leeks, it's easier – just chop them first, then swish gently under cold running water and drain well in a colander.

Makes about 4 cups. PER 1 TBSP: about 31 cal, 1 g pro, 3 g total fat (2 g sat. fat), 1 g carb, trace fibre, 8 mg chol, 79 mg sodium, 22 mg potassium. % RDI: 2% calcium, 1% iron, 3% vit A, 2% folate.

Blue Cheese & Fruit Terrine

The trick to this terrine is to gently mix the cheeses just until combined. You can use any blue-veined cheese, even if it's soft and creamy like Gorgonzola. Just keep it cold, and pull it apart instead of crumbling it.

10 oz (280 g) **blue cheese,** crumbled

1 pkg (5 oz/142 g) **soft goat cheese,** crumbled

⅓ cup finely chopped **dried apricots**

¼ cup finely chopped **dried pears**

¼ cup finely chopped **prunes**

2 tbsp **liquid honey**

4 tsp **brandy**

¾ tsp chopped **fresh thyme**

Pinch **pepper**

½ cup **walnut halves**

½ cup **natural almonds**

Line 8- x 4-inch (1.5 L) loaf pan with plastic wrap, leaving enough overhang to cover top. Set aside.

In large bowl, combine blue cheese, goat cheese, apricots, pears and prunes. Drizzle with 4 tsp of the honey and the brandy; sprinkle with thyme and pepper. Gently toss to combine. Scrape into prepared pan; fold plastic wrap overhang over top to cover completely. Press down gently to compact. Refrigerate for 1 hour. *(Make-ahead: Refrigerate for up to 2 days.)*

Meanwhile, in dry skillet, toast walnuts and almonds over medium-low heat, shaking pan often, until fragrant, about 5 minutes. Let cool.

Turn out terrine onto serving plate; remove plastic wrap. Surround with walnuts and almonds; drizzle with remaining honey.

45

Makes 10 servings. PER SERVING: about 261 cal, 11 g pro, 18 g total fat (8 g sat. fat), 15 g carb, 2 g fibre, 28 mg chol, 451 mg sodium, 251 mg potassium. % RDI: 18% calcium, 8% iron, 12% vit A, 2% vit C, 9% folate.

Potted Cheddar With Port

Classic English potted cheese is an ideal make-ahead appetizer for a busy party season. If you like, split it between two pots to give as gifts.

12 oz (340 g) **aged Cheddar cheese,** cubed and at room temperature

⅓ cup **unsalted butter,** softened

¼ cup **tawny Port**

½ tsp crumbled **dried sage**

¼ tsp **ground mace** (or pinch nutmeg)

Pinch each **salt** and **cayenne pepper**

In food processor, purée Cheddar cheese, butter, Port, sage, mace, salt and cayenne pepper until smooth, scraping down side of bowl often.

Scrape into pot; smooth top. Cover with plastic wrap and refrigerate for up to 2 weeks. *(Make-ahead: To store longer, cover cheese mixture with clarified butter; see How-To, below. Cover with plastic wrap and refrigerate for up to 2 months.)*

Bring to room temperature to serve.

46

How-To

CLARIFYING BUTTER

In saucepan, melt butter over low heat; let cool for 5 minutes. Skim off froth; strain through double-thickness cheesecloth into bowl. Refrigerate until clarified butter solidifies and milky liquid settles at bottom. Discard milky liquid. Remelt and pour over potted cheese.

Makes about 2 cups. PER 1 TBSP: about 61 cal, 3 g pro, 5 g total fat (4 g sat. fat), trace carb, 0 g fibre, 16 mg chol, 66 mg sodium, 13 mg potassium. % RDI: 7% calcium, 1% iron, 5% vit A, 1% folate.

Parmigiano Sun-Dried Tomato Dip

Real Parmigiano-Reggiano cheese gives this dip the richest taste. Yellow peppers, zucchini and blanched green beans are delicious for dipping.

¾ cup **sour cream**

⅔ cup **mayonnaise**

2 tsp **lemon juice**

1 cup grated **Parmigiano-Reggiano cheese**

⅓ cup finely chopped drained **oil-packed sun-dried tomatoes**

¼ cup minced **fresh chives** or green onions

¼ tsp **pepper**

In bowl, whisk together sour cream, mayonnaise and lemon juice; whisk in cheese, tomatoes, chives and pepper.

Cover and refrigerate for 1 hour before serving. *(Make-ahead: Refrigerate for up to 5 days.)*

How-To

USING DRY-PACKED SUN-DRIED TOMATOES

Dry-packed sun-dried tomatoes are handy to keep in your pantry, because they keep for a long time. To substitute them for oil-packed sun-dried tomatoes, soak them in warm water for 10 minutes, then drain and chop as directed.

47

Makes about 2 cups. PER 1 TBSP: about 57 cal, 1 g pro, 5 g total fat (2 g sat. fat), 1 g carb, 0 g fibre, 7 mg chol, 79 mg sodium. % RDI: 4% calcium, 1% iron, 2% vit A, 3% vit C, 1% folate.

Smoked Trout & Salmon Rillette

Smoked fish lovers won't be able to get enough of this appetizer. It takes only a few minutes to make and looks so impressive. Instead of microwaving, you can cook the salmon in a little oil in a skillet over medium heat.

8 oz (225 g) **skinless salmon fillet**

Pinch **salt**

⅓ cup **butter,** melted and cooled

2 tbsp **olive oil**

3 tbsp finely chopped **green onion**

2 tbsp finely chopped drained **capers**

4 tsp chopped **fresh parsley**

4 tsp **lemon juice**

6 oz (170 g) **smoked trout,** skinned

¼ tsp each **pepper** and **sweet paprika**

GARLIC CHIPS AND CROSTINI:

⅓ cup **olive oil**

4 large cloves **garlic,** thinly sliced

1 **baguette,** thinly sliced

GARLIC CHIPS AND CROSTINI: In small saucepan, heat oil over medium-low heat; fry garlic until golden and crisp, about 3 minutes. With slotted spoon, transfer to paper towel–lined plate. Brush 1 side of baguette slices with oil in pan; place on baking sheet. Bake in 350°F (180°C) oven, turning once, until golden, 10 minutes. *(Make-ahead: Store in airtight container for up to 4 days.)*

Sprinkle salmon with salt; microwave on high until fish flakes easily when tested with fork, about 2 minutes. Pat dry with paper towel.

In bowl, stir butter with oil; stir in green onion, capers, parsley and lemon juice. Flake salmon and trout; stir into butter mixture along with pepper and paprika.

Scrape into serving dish; cover and chill for 30 minutes. *(Make-ahead: Refrigerate for up to 2 days. Let stand at room temperature for 30 minutes before serving.)*

Serve on crostini topped with garlic chips.

48

Makes 8 to 10 servings. PER EACH OF 10 SERVINGS: about 291 cal, 12 g pro, 20 g total fat (6 g sat. fat), 15 g carb, 1 g fibre, 42 mg chol, 618 mg sodium, 221 mg potassium. % RDI: 3% calcium, 6% iron, 10% vit A, 6% vit C, 16% folate.

Crab & Three-Cheese Fondue

Keep this sumptuous fondue warm over low heat in a fondue pot or small slow cooker so the mixture doesn't bubble too much and stick to the bottom. Serve with crackers, Lavash (page 133) or Crostini (page 131).

10 oz (280 g) **Brie cheese** or Camembert cheese

1 pkg (250 g) **cream cheese**

2 pkg (each 7 oz/200 g) **frozen crabmeat,** thawed

1 tbsp **butter**

6 **green onions,** thinly sliced

1 clove **garlic,** minced

½ cup **whipping cream** (35%)

¼ cup **dry white wine**

1 tbsp **Dijon mustard**

½ tsp **hot pepper sauce**

½ cup grated **Parmesan cheese**

Cut rind off Brie cheese; cut Brie and cream cheese into small cubes. Cover and let come to room temperature, about 20 minutes.

Drain crabmeat in sieve; pick through and discard any shell or cartilage. Press to remove as much liquid as possible; set aside.

In large skillet, heat butter over medium heat; fry green onions and garlic, stirring often, until softened, about 5 minutes.

Stir in Brie, cream cheese, cream, wine, mustard and hot pepper sauce; cook, mashing with back of spoon and stirring constantly, just until melted.

Remove from heat; stir in crab and Parmesan cheese. Scrape into fondue pot; keep warm over low heat. *(Make-ahead: Let cool. Cover and refrigerate for up to 24 hours. Reheat to serve.)*

50

Makes about 3½ cups. PER 1 TBSP: about 47 cal, 3 g pro, 4 g total fat (2 g sat. fat), trace carb, 0 g fibre, 16 mg chol, 107 mg sodium. % RDI: 2% calcium, 2% iron, 4% vit A, 2% folate.

Tuna, Shrimp & Vegetable Antipasto

The best antipasti are simple, savoury and versatile. This creative combination works on cheese and crackers at a cocktail party, as part of an antipasto platter or in a sandwich.

2 tbsp **extra-virgin olive oil**

1½ cups tiny **cauliflower florets**

1 cup chopped **onion**

2 cloves **garlic,** minced

1 cup chopped **mushrooms**

¼ tsp **pepper**

1 cup **ketchup**

½ cup pitted **black olives,** finely chopped

½ cup **pimiento-stuffed green olives,** finely chopped

½ cup finely chopped **sweet green pepper**

1 can (170 g) **solid white tuna,** drained

1 can (106 g) **small shrimp,** drained

¼ cup **white wine vinegar**

¼ cup chopped **fresh parsley**

In large saucepan, heat oil over medium heat; cook cauliflower, onion, garlic, mushrooms and pepper, stirring occasionally, until onion is softened, about 4 minutes.

Add ketchup, black and green olives, green pepper, tuna, shrimp and vinegar; bring to boil. Reduce heat and simmer, stirring occasionally, until thickened enough to mound on spoon, about 20 minutes. Stir in parsley. *(Make-ahead: Let cool. Refrigerate in airtight container for up to 2 days or freeze for up to 1 month.)*

51

Makes about 4 cups. PER 1 TBSP: about 18 cal, 1 g pro, 1 g total fat (trace sat. fat), 2 g carb, trace fibre, 3 mg chol, 107 mg sodium. % RDI: 1% calcium, 1% iron, 1% vit A, 5% vit C, 1% folate.

Two-Salmon Mousse
(opposite) and
Lavash (page 133)

Two-Salmon Mousse

This recipe makes two mousses, so you can switch plates halfway through the evening and offer your guests a fresh one. If available, choose cold-smoked wild Pacific salmon for its wonderful flavour and vibrant colour.

10 oz (280 g) **boneless skinless salmon fillet**

1 pkg (7 g) **unflavoured gelatin**

2 tbsp **lemon juice**

¼ cup **boiling water**

⅓ cup **light mayonnaise**

1 tbsp **prepared horseradish**

½ tsp each **salt** and **pepper**

1 pkg (150 g) **cold-smoked salmon,** chopped

¼ cup rinsed drained **capers,** coarsely chopped

¼ cup chopped **fresh dill**

¾ cup **whipping cream** (35%)

Place salmon fillet in greased steamer basket over 1 inch (2.5 cm) boiling water. Cover, reduce heat and simmer until fish is opaque when tested, about 8 minutes.

Meanwhile, in bowl, sprinkle gelatin over lemon juice; let stand for 5 minutes to soften. Stir in boiling water until gelatin is dissolved.

In food processor, combine steamed salmon, mayonnaise, horseradish, salt and pepper; pour in gelatin mixture. Blend until puréed; scrape into large bowl. Refrigerate until slightly thickened, about 15 minutes. Stir in smoked salmon, capers and dill.

53

Whip cream; fold into salmon mixture in 2 additions. Pack into 2 plastic wrap–lined 4-cup (1 L) bowls. Cover and refrigerate until firm, about 2 hours. *(Make-ahead: Refrigerate for up to 2 days.)*

Uncover and invert onto serving plate; remove plastic wrap.

Makes 6 cups. PER 1 TBSP: about 16 cal, 1 g pro, 1 g total fat (1 g sat. fat), trace carb, 0 g fibre, 4 mg chol, 43 mg sodium. % RDI: 1% vit A.

Smoked Salmon & Artichoke Dip

Easy to assemble and made mostly from pantry ingredients, this addictive dip is ideal for a crowd any time of year. Serve with puff pastry twists, flatbread, sliced vegetables or even thick-cut potato chips.

3½ oz (100 g) **smoked salmon**

½ cup drained **canned water-packed artichoke hearts**

¼ cup diced **red onion**

¼ cup **light mayonnaise**

¼ cup **light sour cream**

1 tbsp drained **capers**

1 tsp **Dijon mustard**

½ tsp grated **lemon zest**

¼ tsp **pepper**

¼ cup finely chopped **fresh chives**

In food processor, pulse together salmon, artichoke hearts, onion, mayonnaise, sour cream, capers, Dijon mustard, lemon zest and pepper until blended but still chunky.

Stir in chives. *(Make-ahead: Refrigerate in airtight container for up to 3 days.)*

54

Know Your Ingredients

HOT-SMOKED VS. COLD-SMOKED SALMON

Cold-smoked salmon, also called lox, is soft and delicate in texture. It usually comes already sliced and is available in the freezer section of your grocery store. Hot-smoked salmon has a cooked appearance and is usually sold in chunks at the fish counter. It flakes easily and is a bit drier and chewier than cold-smoked salmon. Either type will work in the above dip.

Makes about 1½ cups. PER 1 TBSP: about 19 cal, 1 g pro, 1 g total fat (trace sat. fat), 1 g carb, trace fibre, 2 mg chol, 77 mg sodium, 31 mg potassium. % RDI: 1% calcium, 1% iron, 1% vit A, 2% vit C, 1% folate.

Creamy Shrimp Spread

Shrimp are a party favourite, but they can be expensive. This flavourful spread stretches a smaller amount of shrimp to feed a crowd. For an extra-special presentation, serve in endive leaves and top with shrimp.

8 oz (225 g) cooked deveined peeled **small shrimp**

1 pkg (250 g) **light cream cheese,** softened

4 tsp **lemon juice**

1 tbsp chopped **fresh dill**

1 tbsp **Dijon mustard**

1 tsp **prepared horseradish**

Pinch each **salt** and **pepper**

Fresh dill sprigs

Line 1¼-cup (300 mL) bowl with plastic wrap. Set aside 4 shrimp for garnish.

In food processor, purée together remaining shrimp, cream cheese, lemon juice, dill, Dijon mustard, horseradish, salt and pepper until almost smooth.

Spoon mixture into prepared bowl; press down gently. Cover and refrigerate for 3 hours. *(Make-ahead: Refrigerate for up to 24 hours.)*

Invert onto serving plate; remove plastic wrap. Garnish with reserved shrimp and dill sprigs.

55

Makes 2 cups. PER 1 TBSP: about 26 cal, 2 g pro, 2 g total fat (1 g sat. fat), trace carb, trace fibre, 21 mg chol, 58 mg sodium. % RDI: 1% calcium, 1% iron, 1% vit A, 1% folate.

CHAPTER 3

HOT appetizers

From left: Prosciutto Scallops
(page 82) and Swedish Meatballs
With Rich Gravy (page 59)

57

Pepper-Crusted Beef Bites

These tender cubes of beef with a tangy dipping sauce are elegant and so savoury. Invest in some pretty, frilly toothpicks for spearing.

2 tsp **black peppercorns**

½ tsp **coarse salt**

1 lb (450 g) **beef tenderloin grilling steak,** or rib eye or strip loin grilling steak, cut in 1-inch (2.5 cm) cubes

1 tsp **vegetable oil**

GREEN ONION SOY DIPPING SAUCE:

2 tbsp **soy sauce**

1 tbsp **unseasoned rice vinegar**

1 tsp **sesame oil**

2 tbsp thinly sliced **green onion**

58

GREEN ONION SOY DIPPING SAUCE: Stir together soy sauce, vinegar and sesame oil. *(Make-ahead: Cover and refrigerate for up to 1 day.)* Stir in green onion.

With side of knife or bottom of heavy pan, crush peppercorns until coarse; transfer to bowl and mix with salt. Dip 1 side of each beef cube into pepper mixture, pressing to adhere.

Heat large cast-iron or heavy skillet over medium-high heat; brush with some of the oil. Cook beef in batches, pepper side down and brushing with more oil as needed, until bottom is browned, 2 minutes. Turn; cook until browned on opposite side, 1 minute for rare, 2 minutes for medium-rare. Transfer to warmed platter; serve with dipping sauce.

Makes about 32 pieces. PER PIECE: about 23 cal, 3 g pro, 1 g total fat (trace sat. fat), trace carb, 0 g fibre, 6 mg chol, 106 mg sodium. % RDI: 3% iron.

Swedish Meatballs With Rich Gravy

No holiday spread is complete without meatballs. Preparing them a day ahead means you'll have very little to do at the last minute.

½ cup **fresh bread crumbs**

1 **onion,** grated

3 tbsp **milk**

1 **egg**

½ tsp **salt**

¼ tsp each **ground allspice** and **pepper**

1 lb (450 g) **lean ground beef**

1 lb (450 g) **lean ground pork**

1 tbsp each **vegetable oil** and **butter**

2 tbsp **all-purpose flour**

1 cup **sodium-reduced beef broth**

¼ cup **whipping cream** (35%)

¼ cup **lingonberry jelly** or red currant jelly

In large bowl, stir together bread crumbs, onion, milk, egg, salt, allspice and pepper. Stir in beef and pork until well combined.

Form by rounded 1 tbsp into 36 balls. *(Make-ahead: Cover and refrigerate on parchment paper–lined baking sheet for up to 24 hours.)*

In large skillet, heat oil with butter over medium heat; cook meatballs, in batches and turning often, until golden and instant-read thermometer inserted into centre of several reads 160°F (71°C), 8 to 10 minutes. Transfer to plate.

Drain all but 2 tbsp fat from pan. Stir in flour; cook, stirring, for 1 minute. Stir in broth and ½ cup water; boil, stirring occasionally, for 2 minutes. Stir in cream and jelly; boil, stirring, for 1 minute.

Return meatballs and any accumulated juices to pan; simmer for 3 minutes.

59

Makes 10 to 12 servings. PER EACH OF 12 SERVINGS: about 223 cal, 16 g pro, 13 g total fat (5 g sat. fat), 11 g carb, trace fibre, 68 mg chol, 240 mg sodium, 238 mg potassium. % RDI: 3% calcium, 10% iron, 3% vit A, 7% folate.

Thai Pork Skewers

This curry-scented marinade uses only a bit of Thai red curry paste, but an opened jar will keep in the fridge for up to one year. Try the luscious peanut sauce on grilled chicken as well.

1 **pork tenderloin,** trimmed (about 1 lb/450 g)

MARINADE:

2 tbsp packed **brown sugar**

2 tbsp chopped **fresh cilantro** or parsley

2 tbsp **lime juice**

2 cloves **garlic,** minced

1 tbsp grated **fresh ginger**

1 tbsp **sodium-reduced soy sauce**

1 tsp **Thai red curry paste**

PEANUT SAUCE:

⅓ cup **natural peanut butter**

⅓ cup **coconut milk**

2 tbsp **lime juice**

1 tbsp **sodium-reduced soy sauce**

1 tsp packed **brown sugar**

½ tsp **hot pepper sauce**

PEANUT SAUCE: In food processor, blend together peanut butter, coconut milk, lime juice, soy sauce, brown sugar and hot pepper sauce until smooth. Pour into bowl; cover and set aside.

Cut pork into twenty-six 3- x ½- x ¼-inch (8 x 1 cm x 5 mm) strips.

MARINADE: In large bowl, whisk together brown sugar, cilantro, lime juice, garlic, ginger, soy sauce and curry paste; add pork, tossing to coat. Cover and refrigerate for 4 hours. *(Make-ahead: Refrigerate peanut sauce and pork separately for up to 24 hours. Bring sauce to room temperature, thinning with up to 2 tbsp water, if desired.)*

Thread pork onto small metal or soaked wooden skewers; place on broiler pan or foil-lined rimmed baking sheet. Broil, 6 inches (15 cm) from heat and turning once, until lightly browned and no longer pink inside, about 6 minutes. Serve with peanut sauce for dipping.

60

Makes 26 pieces. PER PIECE: about 56 cal, 5 g pro, 3 g total fat (1 g sat. fat), 2 g carb, trace fibre, 9 mg chol, 56 mg sodium. % RDI: 1% calcium, 4% iron, 1% folate.

Dijon Rosemary Lamb Lolli-Chops

These small chops are ideal finger food: they come with built-in handles! Look for frozen frenched lamb racks or ask your butcher to french the racks (remove the chine bone and fat, then scrape the bones clean).

4 **frenched racks of lamb** (2¾ lb/1.2 kg total)

2 tbsp chopped **fresh rosemary**

1 tbsp **extra-virgin olive oil**

2 cloves **garlic,** minced

1½ tsp crushed **fennel seeds**

½ tsp each **salt** and **pepper**

¼ cup **Dijon mustard**

1 tbsp **lemon juice**

62

Trim any fat off lamb; scrape bones to remove any remaining bits of meat.

Combine rosemary, oil, garlic, fennel seeds, salt and pepper; rub over lamb, avoiding exposed bones. *(Make-ahead: Wrap in plastic wrap and refrigerate for up to 24 hours.)*

Stir Dijon mustard with lemon juice; spread on meaty side of lamb, avoiding bones.

Roast lamb, meaty side up, on foil-lined baking sheet in 450°F (230°C) oven until medium-rare and instant-read thermometer inserted into centre reads 145°F (63°C), about 20 minutes. Transfer to carving board; tent with foil. Let stand for 10 minutes before slicing between bones into chops.

Makes about 24 pieces. PER PIECE: about 43 cal, 5 g pro, 3 g total fat (1 g sat. fat), trace carb, trace fibre, 16 mg chol, 90 mg sodium, 34 mg potassium. % RDI: 1% calcium, 3% iron.

Orange Caramel–Glazed Beef & Green Onion Rolls

These nibbles of tender beef rolled around crunchy green onions are glazed with a vibrant orange sweet-and-sour sauce.

1 lb (450 g) **top sirloin grilling steak,** 1 inch (2.5 cm) thick

1 tbsp grated **fresh ginger**

1 tsp **sesame oil**

6 **green onions**

1 tbsp **vegetable oil**

ORANGE CARAMEL GLAZE:

1 tsp grated **orange zest**

¼ cup **orange juice**

2 tbsp **soy sauce**

1 tbsp **sesame oil**

2 tbsp **granulated sugar**

Pinch **hot pepper flakes**

1 tsp **cornstarch**

ORANGE CARAMEL GLAZE: Combine orange zest, orange juice and soy sauce; set aside. In small saucepan, heat sesame oil over medium-high heat; add sugar and cook, stirring, until beginning to colour, about 1 minute. Add hot pepper flakes; cook until deep chestnut colour, about 1 minute. Immediately remove from heat. Averting eyes, stir in orange juice mixture. Return to simmer. Mix cornstarch with 1 tbsp water; add to pan and cook, stirring, until thickened. Set aside. *(Make-ahead: Refrigerate in airtight container for up to 24 hours. Reheat to serve.)*

Trim fat from steak. With knife held at 45-degree angle, cut steak crosswise into 6 equal parts. With meat pounder, pound each until 6 inches (15 cm) long, 3 inches (8 cm) wide and ¼ inch (5 mm) thick.

Mix ginger with sesame oil; rub over steak. Arrange 1 green onion lengthwise down each slice; trim off overhanging green part. Roll steak around onion; secure with toothpicks. *(Make-ahead: Cover and refrigerate for up to 6 hours.)*

In skillet, heat vegetable oil over high heat; cook rolls, turning once, for 2 minutes per side. Cut each into 5 pieces; secure each with toothpick. Arrange on serving plate; spoon glaze over top.

63

Makes 30 pieces. PER PIECE: about 33 cal, 3 g pro, 2 g total fat (trace sat. fat), 2 g carb, trace fibre, 7 mg chol, 75 mg sodium. % RDI: 3% iron, 2% vit C, 1% folate.

Chinese Sticky Chicken Wings

Talk about finger-licking good. These wings are sweet and well spiced, thanks to the five-spice powder. If you don't have any, substitute ½ tsp cinnamon and pinch each ground cloves and pepper.

½ cup **granulated sugar**

3 tbsp **sodium-reduced soy sauce** or tamari

1 tbsp **unseasoned rice vinegar** or cider vinegar

¾ tsp **five-spice powder**

1½ lb (675 g) **chicken wings** (tips removed)

¼ tsp **white pepper**

1 cup **vegetable oil**

3 **green onions,** cut in 1½-inch (4 cm) pieces

2 cloves **garlic,** minced

1 **hot red pepper** (optional), seeded and thinly sliced

In heavy-bottom saucepan, heat sugar over medium heat, swirling occasionally but not stirring, until melted, clear and nutty brown. Remove from heat. Averting face, stir in soy sauce and vinegar until bubbles subside; stir in five-spice powder. If mixture clumps, stir over low heat until almost melted (any remaining clumps will melt during cooking). Set aside.

Sprinkle wings with white pepper. In wok or skillet, heat oil over medium-high heat; fry wings, in 2 batches, until golden and juices run clear when chicken is pierced, about 6 minutes per batch. Drain in sieve over heatproof bowl; discard oil.

Reserving 1½ tbsp, drain oil from wok; wipe clean. Return reserved oil to wok and heat over medium-high heat; fry green onions and garlic until fragrant, about 30 seconds.

Add wings, and hot pepper (if using); stir-fry for 1 minute. Add caramel mixture; stir-fry until reduced and wings are coated, about 2 minutes.

65

Makes about 15 pieces. PER PIECE: about 79 cal, 4 g pro, 4 g total fat (1 g sat. fat), 8 g carb, trace fibre, 17 mg chol, 137 mg sodium, 61 mg potassium. % RDI: 1% calcium, 3% iron, 1% vit A, 7% vit C, 2% folate.

Pineapple-Glazed Tiki Ribs

A little retro (remember pupu platters?) and a lot delicious, these ribs are a perfect addition to a tropical-themed party menu.

2 lb (900 g) **pork ribs** (spare, side or back)

2 tbsp **soy sauce**

2 tbsp minced **garlic**

1 tsp **ground coriander**

1 tsp **five-spice powder**

¼ tsp **pepper**

½ cup **pineapple juice concentrate**

2 tbsp **granulated sugar**

2 tbsp **malt syrup** or liquid honey

4 tsp **dry mustard**

2 tsp **Worcestershire sauce**

2 tsp **unseasoned rice vinegar**

Cut rib racks in half; arrange in single layer in 13- x 9-inch (3 L) baking dish. Sprinkle with soy sauce, turning to coat; let stand for 2 minutes.

Combine garlic, coriander, five-spice powder and pepper; rub all over ribs. Turn meat side up; cover with foil. Roast in 375°F (190°C) oven for 1 hour.

Meanwhile, in small saucepan, bring pineapple juice concentrate, sugar, malt syrup, mustard, Worcestershire sauce and vinegar to boil; boil over medium-high heat until reduced by about half, 4 to 5 minutes.

Drain fat from ribs; brush with about one-third of the warm pineapple glaze. Roast, uncovered, for 35 minutes, turning and brushing with remaining glaze twice.

Let stand for 5 minutes before cutting into single-rib portions.

66

Makes 6 to 8 servings. PER EACH OF 8 SERVINGS: about 259 cal, 16 g pro, 14 g total fat (5 g sat. fat), 17 g carb, trace fibre, 55 mg chol, 279 mg sodium, 231 mg potassium. % RDI: 3% calcium, 10% iron, 10% vit C, 3% folate.

Buffalo-Style Wings With Blue Cheese Dip & Crudités

Frank's RedHot Original hot sauce is *the* hot sauce for this classic, but you can try other brands, adjusting the amount as desired.

⅓ cup **butter**

⅔ cup **Frank's RedHot Original hot sauce**

4 tsp **cider vinegar**

½ tsp **salt**

3 lb (1.35 kg) **chicken wings** (tips removed)

Vegetable oil for deep-frying

6 cups **vegetable crudités** (such as carrot and celery sticks)

2 batches **Blue Cheese Dip** (page 39)

In small saucepan, melt butter over medium heat; stir in hot sauce, vinegar and salt. Set aside and keep warm.

Separate wings at joint. Pour enough oil into deep-fryer or large wide heavy-bottomed pot to come at least 2½ inches (6 cm) but no more than halfway up side of pot. Heat over medium heat until deep-fry thermometer reads 375°F (190°C).

Deep-fry wings, in 2 batches, until crisp, floating and juices run clear when wings are pierced, 10 to 12 minutes per batch. With slotted spoon, transfer to paper towel–lined bowl.

Discard paper towels; pour sauce over wings, tossing to coat. Serve with vegetables and dip.

67

How-To

MAKING WINGS EXTRA-CRISPY

For extra-crispy wings, after tossing them with sauce, roast on foil-lined baking sheet in 400°F (200°C) oven until sauce clings to wings, about 8 minutes.

Makes about 30 pieces. PER PIECE (WITHOUT VEGETABLES AND DIP): about 62 cal, 4 g pro, 5 g total fat (2 g sat. fat), trace carb, 0 g fibre, 21 mg chol, 255 mg sodium. % RDI: 2% iron, 3% vit A, 1% vit C, 1% folate.

Shrimp & Leek Dumplings

Chinese dumpling (*jiaozi*) wrappers are white, round and thicker than wonton wrappers. Dip the dumplings in a mixture of equal parts Chinese red or black vinegar and soy sauce sprinkled with thinly sliced green onion.

45 **dumpling wrappers**

¼ cup **peanut oil** or vegetable oil (approx)

SHRIMP & LEEK FILLING:

2 cups minced **leeks** (white and light green parts only)

1 tsp **salt**

1 lb (450 g) **raw shrimp,** peeled and deveined

3 oz (85 g) **ground pork**

1 **egg yolk**

¼ cup finely chopped **fresh cilantro**

2 tsp **light soy sauce** or sodium-reduced soy sauce

2 tsp **Chinese rice wine,** dry sherry or sake

1 tsp grated **fresh ginger**

1 tsp **fish sauce** or light soy sauce

1 tsp **sesame oil**

Pinch **white pepper** or black pepper

SHRIMP & LEEK FILLING: Toss leeks with salt; let stand for 30 minutes. Squeeze out moisture. Transfer to large bowl. On cutting board and using side of cleaver, pound 1 shrimp until pulpy; chop a few times and add to bowl. Repeat with remaining shrimp. Mix in pork, egg yolk, cilantro, soy sauce, Chinese rice wine, ginger, fish sauce, sesame oil and white pepper.

For each dumpling, with finger, wet edge of 1 wrapper with water. Place about 2½ tsp filling in centre; fold wrapper over and pinch edge together. Pleat edge, pinching to secure. Stand on cornstarch-dusted tray; cover with tea towel.

For each of about 4 batches, add 1 tbsp peanut oil to cast-iron or nonstick skillet; add enough dumplings to fit snugly without touching. Heat over medium-high heat until oil sizzles; pour in ½ cup water. Cover and cook until dry and spattering ceases; uncover and cook, if necessary, until bottoms are golden.

Change It Up

PORK DUMPLING FILLING

Toss 3 cups finely chopped napa cabbage (8 oz/225 g) with 1 tsp salt; let stand for 20 minutes. Squeeze out moisture. Transfer to large bowl. Mix in 1 lb (450 g) lean ground pork; ½ cup minced green onion; 1 egg, beaten; 1 tbsp soy sauce; 1 tsp grated fresh ginger; 1 tsp sesame oil; ¼ tsp white or black pepper; and pinch cayenne pepper. Prepare dumplings as directed. **Makes about 3 cups, enough for about 60 dumplings.**

Makes 45 dumplings. PER DUMPLING: about 54 cal, 3 g pro, 2 g total fat (trace sat. fat), 6 g carb, trace fibre, 18 mg chol, 111 mg sodium, 34 mg potassium. % RDI: 1% calcium, 4% iron, 1% vit A, 5% folate.

68

Chinese-Style Meatballs

You can either serve the hoisin dip alongside the meatballs or toss it with them. Sambal oelek is an Asian condiment, available in many supermarkets and specialty stores.

1 can (8 oz/227 mL) **whole water chestnuts,** drained

2 **eggs**

¼ cup chopped **fresh cilantro**

2 **green onions,** thinly sliced

3 cloves **garlic,** minced

2 **green finger hot peppers,** seeded and finely chopped

3 tbsp **cornstarch**

2 tbsp **soy sauce**

1 tsp minced **fresh ginger**

¼ tsp **salt**

¼ tsp **white pepper** or black pepper

1 lb (450 g) **lean ground veal**

1 lb (450 g) **lean ground pork**

HOISIN DIP:

⅓ cup **sodium-reduced chicken broth** or vegetable broth

⅓ cup **hoisin sauce**

2 tsp **sambal oelek**

1½ tsp **sesame oil**

On cutting board and with side of knife, smash water chestnuts; coarsely chop and set aside.

In bowl, whisk together eggs, cilantro, green onions, garlic, hot peppers, cornstarch, soy sauce, ginger, salt and white pepper. Mix in veal, pork and water chestnuts. Shape by about 1 tbsp into balls; arrange on foil-lined baking sheet. *(Make-ahead: Cover and refrigerate for up to 24 hours.)*

Bake in 375°F (190°C) oven until instant-read thermometer inserted into several meatballs reads 160°F (71°C), about 15 minutes.

HOISIN DIP: In small saucepan, bring chicken broth to boil over medium-high heat. Remove pan from heat; whisk in hoisin sauce, sambal oelek and sesame oil. Serve with meatballs.

70

Makes about 70 pieces. PER PIECE: about 28 cal, 3 g pro, 1 g total fat (1 g sat. fat), 1 g carb, trace fibre, 15 mg chol, 79 mg sodium, 43 mg potassium. % RDI: 1% iron, 1% folate.

Tortilla, Spinach & Bacon Roll-Ups

For a Spanish twist, use manchego cheese instead of the Monterey Jack.

1 tsp **extra-virgin olive oil**

Half small **red onion,** sliced

1 bag (10 oz/284 g) **fresh spinach,** trimmed

1½ cups **cream cheese,** softened

3 tbsp minced **fresh cilantro**

1 tbsp minced **jalapeño pepper**

½ tsp **pepper**

¼ tsp **salt**

10 **small tortillas**

1 cup shredded **Monterey Jack cheese**

8 slices **bacon,** cooked and crumbled

In skillet, heat oil over medium heat; fry onion just until softened, about 2 minutes. Transfer to bowl.

Rinse spinach; shake off excess water. In large saucepan or Dutch oven, cook spinach, with just the water clinging to leaves, over medium-high heat, stirring occasionally, until wilted, about 5 minutes. Transfer to sieve and let cool; press out moisture. Chop spinach; add to onion.

Beat together cream cheese, cilantro, jalapeño pepper, pepper and salt until smooth. Divide among tortillas, spreading evenly. Top with spinach mixture, leaving 2 inches (5 cm) cream cheese uncovered on 1 side. Sprinkle Monterey Jack cheese and bacon over spinach. Roll up toward uncovered cream cheese; press to seal. Place, seam side down, on tray. Refrigerate until firm, about 1 hour.

Trim ends of each tortilla. Cut each roll into 6 slices; place, cut side down, on foil-lined rimmed baking sheet. *(Make-ahead: Freeze until firm, about 1 hour. Layer between waxed paper in airtight container and freeze for up to 1 month. Cook from frozen, adding 1 minute to broiling time and turning halfway through.)*

Broil, 8 inches (20 cm) from heat, until golden and cheese is melted, about 3 minutes.

71

Makes 60 pieces. PER PIECE: about 51 cal, 1 g pro, 3 g total fat (2 g sat. fat), 3 g carb, trace fibre, 9 mg chol, 78 mg sodium. % RDI: 2% calcium, 3% iron, 6% vit A, 2% vit C, 6% folate.

Cajun Crab Cakes

Crisp outside and tender inside, these bites have just a hint of heat. If you make and freeze a batch ahead, they'll need only a quick sauté to be ready.

2 pkg (each 7 oz/200 g) **frozen crabmeat,** thawed

1⅓ cups crushed **unsalted soda crackers** (about 35)

1 cup **light mayonnaise**

¼ cup each finely diced **carrot** and **sweet green pepper**

¼ cup grated **radishes**

¼ cup finely chopped **green onions**

1 tbsp **Cajun seasoning**

1 tbsp **Dijon mustard**

1 tsp **hot pepper sauce**

¼ tsp each **salt** and **pepper**

2 tbsp **vegetable oil**

CHIVE SOUR CREAM:

½ cup **light sour cream**

2 tbsp chopped **fresh chives**

Place crabmeat in sieve; pick through and discard any shell or cartilage. Press firmly to remove liquid. Transfer to large bowl; stir in crackers, mayonnaise, carrot, green pepper, radishes, green onions, Cajun seasoning, mustard, hot pepper sauce, salt and pepper until combined.

Press by heaping 1 tbsp into ½-inch (1 cm) thick patties. *(Make-ahead: Freeze on baking sheet until firm, about 2 hours. Layer between waxed paper in airtight container and freeze for up to 2 weeks. Thaw in refrigerator.)*

CHIVE SOUR CREAM: Stir sour cream with chives. Set aside.

In nonstick skillet, heat 1 tbsp of the oil over medium-high heat. Cook crab cakes, in batches and adding more oil as necessary, until golden, 3 minutes per side. Serve with chive sour cream.

73

Makes about 32 pieces. PER PIECE: about 65 cal, 4 g pro, 4 g total fat (trace sat. fat), 4 g carb, trace fibre, 9 mg chol, 199 mg sodium. % RDI: 2% calcium, 4% iron, 4% vit A, 3% vit C, 3% folate.

Lemon Rosemary Chicken Skewers

Mixing a spoonful of mayonnaise with some of the marinade (before you've tossed in the chicken, of course!) makes an excellent dipping sauce for these skewers.

4 **chicken cutlets** (1¼ lb/565 g)

3 tbsp **extra-virgin olive oil**

2 tbsp minced **green onions**
    or fresh chives

4 tsp chopped **fresh rosemary**

2 tsp grated **lemon zest**

1 tbsp **lemon juice**

½ tsp **salt**

¼ tsp **pepper**

3 tbsp **light mayonnaise**

Between plastic wrap, pound chicken to ¼-inch (5 mm) thickness; cut crosswise into about twenty-four 1-inch (2.5 cm) wide strips.

In large bowl, whisk together oil, green onions, rosemary, lemon zest, lemon juice, salt and pepper. Transfer 4 tsp to small bowl; whisk in mayonnaise. Cover and refrigerate sauce.

Add chicken to remaining marinade; toss to coat. Weave 1 strip onto each of 24 soaked 6-inch (15 cm) wooden skewers. Place on greased foil-lined rimmed baking sheet; cover and refrigerate for 1 hour. (*Make-ahead: Refrigerate for up to 2 hours.*)

Broil skewers, 6 inches (15 cm) from heat, until chicken is no longer pink inside, about 5 minutes. Serve with sauce for dipping.

74

Makes about 24 pieces. PER PIECE: about 48 cal, 5 g pro, 3 g total fat (trace sat. fat), trace carb, 0 g fibre, 15 mg chol, 73 mg sodium. % RDI: 1% iron, 2% vit C.

Surf & Turf Skewers

Shrimp are often sold by the number per pound (450 g). Jumbos are usually labelled "21/25," which means there are 21 to 25 shrimp per pound. Use them here, because smaller shrimp won't wrap around the beef.

8 oz (225 g) **beef tenderloin grilling steak**

24 **raw jumbo shrimp** (1 lb/450 g), peeled and deveined

MARINADE:

2 tbsp **extra-virgin olive oil**

1 tbsp chopped **fresh thyme** (or 1 tsp dried)

1 tbsp **sherry vinegar** or red wine vinegar

½ tsp **smoked paprika** or sweet paprika

¼ tsp each **salt** and **pepper**

Trim and cut beef into twenty-four ¾-inch (2 cm) cubes. Thread tail end of 1 shrimp onto small metal or soaked wooden skewer; add beef cube, then skewer body end of shrimp. Repeat to make 24 skewers. *(Make-ahead: Cover and refrigerate for up to 8 hours.)*

MARINADE: In shallow dish, whisk together oil, thyme, vinegar, paprika, salt and pepper; add skewers, turning to coat. Cover and refrigerate for 30 minutes. *(Make-ahead: Refrigerate for up to 2 hours.)*

Arrange skewers on broiler pan or foil-lined rimmed baking sheet. Broil, 6 inches (15 cm) from heat and turning once, until shrimp are pink and opaque and beef is still pink in centre, 4 minutes.

75

Makes 24 pieces. PER PIECE: about 38 cal, 5 g pro, 2 g total fat (trace sat. fat), trace carb, 0 g fibre, 26 mg chol, 49 mg sodium. % RDI: 1% calcium, 4% iron, 1% vit A.

Crispy Calamari

If you're not keen on cleaning fresh squid, ask if your fishmonger or supermarket stocks cleaned frozen squid. Enjoy these golden bites with a squeeze of lemon or dipped into Basil Aïoli (page 18).

1½ lb (675 g) fresh or thawed frozen **squid**

8 cups **canola oil,** safflower oil or other vegetable oil

½ cup **all-purpose flour**

¼ cup **cornstarch**

½ tsp **cayenne pepper**

½ tsp **sea salt** or salt

1 **lemon,** cut in wedges

76

How-To

TESTING OIL TEMPERATURE

No deep-fry thermometer? If oil is hot enough, it should bubble vigorously after dropping in one piece of floured calamari, and calamari should turn golden in 1 to 1½ minutes.

For fresh squid, holding tube, pull off head and tentacles; set aside. Rinse squid tubes under cold water, rubbing off purplish skin. Pull out and discard "pens" (clear long plastic-like skeletons) from centres of tubes. Pull off and discard fins from tubes. Cut off and discard eyes and head from tentacles, keeping tentacles attached on ring on top; squeeze hard beak from centre of tentacles and discard.

Cut squid tubes crosswise into ½-inch (1 cm) wide rings; pat dry. In wok or deep heavy-bottomed pot, heat oil until deep-fry thermometer reads 375°F (190°C).

Meanwhile, in large plastic bag, shake together flour, cornstarch and cayenne pepper. All at once, add squid tentacles and rings to flour mixture; shake to coat. Transfer to sieve; lightly shake off excess flour mixture.

Fry calamari, in batches, until golden, 1 to 1½ minutes. Using slotted spoon, transfer to paper towel–lined plate. Sprinkle with salt just before serving with lemon wedges.

Makes 6 servings. PER SERVING: about 326 cal, 19 g pro, 20 g total fat (2 g sat. fat), 17 g carb, trace fibre, 265 mg chol, 180 mg sodium. % RDI: 4% calcium, 9% iron, 1% vit C, 12% folate.

Smoky Quesadillas

Salsa verde (green salsa) is a mild sauce made from tomatillos and green hot peppers. Look for it in the Mexican section of your supermarket.

½ cup **salsa verde**

¼ cup chopped **fresh cilantro**

1 tbsp **lime juice**

2 tbsp **olive oil**

¾ cup finely chopped **sweet onion**

½ cup finely chopped **sweet green pepper**

Half to whole **jalapeño pepper,** seeded and minced

¼ tsp **salt**

4 large **whole wheat tortillas**

1 cup shredded **smoked Cheddar cheese** or other smoked cheese

2 oz (55 g) thinly sliced **dry-cured Spanish-style salami,** or cured or cooked chorizo sausage

Mix together salsa verde, chopped cilantro and lime juice; set aside.

In nonstick skillet, heat 1 tbsp of the oil over medium heat; fry onion, green pepper, jalapeño pepper and salt, stirring occasionally, until softened, 6 to 8 minutes. Spread half over 1 of the tortillas; top with half each of the cheese and salami. Cover with second tortilla.

In skillet, heat 1 tsp of the remaining oil over medium heat; add quesadilla and drizzle ½ tsp of the remaining oil over top. Fry, turning halfway through, until golden on both sides, 4 to 6 minutes. Cut into 6 wedges. Repeat with remaining tortillas, onion mixture, cheese, salami and oil. Serve with salsa mixture.

78

Makes 12 pieces. PER PIECE: about 148 cal, 6 g pro, 9 g total fat (3 g sat. fat), 12 g carb, 1 g fibre, 14 mg chol, 445 mg sodium, 75 mg potassium. % RDI: 7% calcium, 5% iron, 4% vit A, 9% vit C, 6% folate.

Warm Mixed Olives & Chorizo

This appetizer blends a variety of typical Mediterranean flavours. Many supermarkets have an olive bar in the deli section – try any of your favourite varieties of unpitted green and black olives in this recipe.

4 oz (115 g) **smoked chorizo** or other smoked sausage

Half small **navel orange**

2 tbsp **extra-virgin olive oil**

1 cup **unpitted oil-cured black olives**

1 cup **unpitted brined black olives** (such as Kalamata)

1 cup **unpitted large green olives**

2 cloves **garlic,** thinly sliced

1 tsp **hot pepper flakes**

1 tbsp **fresh sage leaves,** thinly sliced

Slice chorizo into thin rounds; set aside. Thinly slice orange into half-moon shapes; set aside.

In large skillet, heat oil over medium heat; cook chorizo for 1 minute. Add oil-cured and brined black olives, green olives, garlic and hot pepper flakes; cook, stirring occasionally, until warmed through and fragrant, about 3 minutes.

Stir in sage and orange; cook until orange starts to break down, about 2 minutes. Remove from heat; cover and let stand for 10 minutes. Serve warm. *(Make-ahead: Cover and refrigerate for up to 3 days. Reheat to serve.)*

79

Makes 4 cups. PER 2 TBSP: about 61 cal, 1 g pro, 6 g total fat (1 g sat. fat), 2 g carb, 1 g fibre, 3 mg chol, 393 mg sodium, 27 mg potassium. % RDI: 1% calcium, 1% iron, 1% vit A, 3% vit C.

Double-Garlic Baked Shrimp

Roasted and fresh garlic give these tender shrimp rich, deep flavour. Serve with baguette slices to soak up the delicious sauce.

2 cups **grape tomatoes** or cherry tomatoes

1 head **garlic,** separated into cloves and peeled

Half **lemon,** quartered

3 tbsp **olive oil**

½ tsp **salt**

1 lb (450 g) deveined peeled **raw large shrimp**

2 cloves **garlic,** pressed or minced

½ tsp **smoked paprika** or sweet paprika

¼ tsp **dried marjoram** or dried oregano

2 tbsp finely chopped **fresh parsley**

In shallow 8-cup (2 L) baking dish, stir together tomatoes, garlic cloves, lemon, oil and salt. Bake in 425°F (220°C) oven, stirring halfway through, for 30 minutes.

Toss together shrimp, pressed garlic, paprika and marjoram; stir into tomato mixture. Bake until shrimp are pink and opaque, about 7 minutes. Stir in parsley.

81

Makes 4 to 6 servings. PER EACH OF 6 SERVINGS: about 162 cal, 16 g pro, 8 g total fat (1 g sat. fat), 6 g carb, 1 g fibre, 115 mg chol, 308 mg sodium, 311 mg potassium. % RDI: 6% calcium, 16% iron, 9% vit A, 28% vit C, 6% folate.

Prosciutto Scallops

This delicious, simple starter is such a crowd-pleaser that you'll probably want to double the recipe. Or serve a mix of the flavourful variations for guests to sample and enjoy.

4 thin slices **prosciutto**
(about 2 oz/55 g)

20 **sea scallops**
(about 12 oz/340 g)

2 tbsp **lemon juice**

2 tbsp **liquid honey**

Stack prosciutto slices; cut crosswise into 5 stacks to make 20 strips. Pat scallops dry. Place 1 scallop at 1 end of each prosciutto strip; roll up to enclose. Skewer with toothpick. *(Make-ahead: Cover and refrigerate for up to 4 hours.)*

Place scallops on foil-lined rimmed baking sheet. Mix lemon juice with honey; brush over rolls. Bake in 425°F (220°C) oven until scallops are opaque and prosciutto is crisp, about 10 minutes.

Change It Up

PROSCIUTTO SHRIMP

Substitute deveined peeled raw large shrimp for the scallops.

PROSCIUTTO FIGS

Omit scallops. Pour boiling water over 20 plump dried fig halves; let stand for 5 minutes. Drain well. Continue with recipe.

PROSCIUTTO DATES

Omit scallops. Pour boiling water over 20 plump pitted dates; let stand for 5 minutes. Drain well. Continue with recipe.

82

Makes 20 pieces. PER PIECE: about 26 cal, 3 g pro, trace total fat (0 g sat. fat), 2 g carb, 0 g fibre, 7 mg chol, 64 mg sodium. % RDI: 1% iron.

Lobster Cakes With Dilled Crème Fraîche on Greens

An elegant dinner party with a few close friends is the perfect occasion to splurge on the best ingredients. If you don't have time to cook fresh lobsters, use 1 lb (450 g) canned cooked lobster for these delicate cakes.

6 cups **baby salad greens**

2 tbsp **extra-virgin olive oil**

1 tbsp **lemon juice**

Pinch each **salt** and **pepper**

DILLED CRÈME FRAÎCHE:

⅓ cup **crème fraîche**

1 tbsp minced **fresh dill**

LOBSTER CAKES:

2 **cooked lobsters** (each 1½ lb/675 g), shelled (see How-To, below)

½ cup **fresh bread crumbs**

¼ cup finely diced **sweet red pepper**

1 tsp **green onion,** minced

½ tsp grated **lemon zest**

¼ cup **mayonnaise**

2 **egg whites**

Pinch each **salt** and **pepper**

1 tbsp **vegetable oil** (approx)

DILLED CRÈME FRAÎCHE: Stir crème fraîche with dill; set aside. *(Make-ahead: Cover and refrigerate for up to 1 hour.)*

LOBSTER CAKES: Dice lobster meat to make about 2 cups. In bowl, combine lobster, bread crumbs, red pepper, green onion and lemon zest. Stir in mayonnaise, egg whites, salt and pepper. Using scant ¼ cup each, form into 12 patties; place on parchment paper–lined baking sheet. *(Make-ahead: Cover and refrigerate for up to 2 hours.)*

In large nonstick skillet, heat oil over medium-high heat; cook patties, in batches and adding more oil if necessary, until browned on both sides. Return to baking sheet; bake in 375°F (190°C) oven until firm to the touch, about 5 minutes.

Meanwhile, toss together salad greens, olive oil, lemon juice, salt and pepper; divide among 6 plates. Arrange 2 lobster cakes on each; top with dollop of dilled crème fraîche.

83

How-To

COOKING AND SHELLING FRESH LOBSTERS

Fill large pot with enough salted water (1 tbsp salt per 4 cups water) to cover lobsters; bring to rolling boil. Plunge each lobster headfirst into water. Cover; return to boil. Reduce heat; simmer until bright red and small legs tear away easily, 10 minutes. Drain; let cool. Halve lobsters lengthwise. Twist off claws at body joint; separate into claw and arm sections. Break off small part of claw; pick out meat. Crack large part of claw at widest part; lift out meat. Crack arm; pick out meat. Remove meat from tail.

Makes 6 servings. PER SERVING: about 250 cal, 15 g pro, 19 g total fat (5 g sat. fat), 6 g carb, 1 g fibre, 62 mg chol, 330 mg sodium. % RDI: 8% calcium, 6% iron, 20% vit A, 32% vit C, 26% folate.

Sesame Shrimp With Wasabi Sauce

Succulent shrimp in a crispy sesame coating are irresistible. Look for tubes of ready-made wasabi paste in the Asian or sushi sections of supermarkets, or buy it in powder form and mix 4 tsp with 2 tsp water.

½ cup **sesame seeds**

½ cup **fine fresh bread crumbs**

¼ tsp **salt**

2 **egg whites**

1 lb (450 g) **raw large shrimp** (about 30), peeled and deveined, tails intact

WASABI SAUCE:

½ cup **light mayonnaise**

2 tsp **wasabi paste**

1 tbsp **lime juice**

1 tsp **sesame oil**

1 tsp finely chopped **fresh chives** or green onion

WASABI SAUCE: In small bowl, whisk together mayonnaise, wasabi paste, lime juice and sesame oil; stir in chives. Set aside.

In shallow dish, stir together sesame seeds, bread crumbs and salt. In separate small bowl, beat egg whites; add shrimp, turning to coat. Press into sesame mixture to coat all over; place on greased large rimmed baking sheet.

Broil, 4 inches (10 cm) from heat, until shrimp are pink and opaque and coating is golden, about 2 minutes per side. Serve with wasabi sauce.

84

Makes about 40 pieces. PER PIECE: about 44 cal, 3 g pro, 3 g total fat (trace sat. fat), 1 g carb, trace fibre, 19 mg chol, 74 mg sodium. % RDI: 1% calcium, 4% iron, 1% vit A, 2% folate.

Rösti Squares With Bacon & Chives

Bacon and chives are just the beginning. These crispy potato squares are the perfect backdrop for other delectable toppings, such as smoked oysters or salmon, chopped sweet red pepper or minced olives.

5 **baking potatoes** (3 lb/1.35 kg), peeled

2 tbsp **butter,** melted

1 tsp **salt**

¼ tsp **pepper**

6 slices **bacon**

¾ cup **sour cream**

2 tbsp chopped **fresh chives** or green onions

In large pot of boiling salted water, cover and cook potatoes for 10 minutes. Drain; let cool. Using coarse side of box grater, grate potatoes into large bowl. Add butter, salt and pepper; toss to combine.

Line 15- x 10-inch (40 x 25 cm) rimmed baking sheet with parchment paper; firmly press potato mixture evenly into pan. Bake on bottom rack in 500°F (260°C) oven until golden on top and bottom, 45 minutes. Let cool on pan on rack.

Meanwhile, in skillet, cook bacon over medium-high heat until crisp, about 5 minutes. Drain on paper towel–lined plate; let cool. Crumble.

Stir sour cream with chives. Cut rösti into 1½-inch (4 cm) squares; top each with 1 tsp of the sour cream mixture. Sprinkle with bacon.

86

Makes 60 pieces. PER PIECE: about 26 cal, 1 g pro, 1 g total fat (trace sat. fat), 3 g carb, trace fibre, 3 mg chol, 93 mg sodium. % RDI: 1% iron, 1% vit A, 2% vit C, 1% folate.

Mini Golden Latkes

Lacy and crisp, these bite-size latkes are downright addictive. Top with crème fraîche or sour cream and smoked salmon for an ideal appetizer.

10 large **baking potatoes** (about 5 lb/2.25 kg), peeled

2 **onions,** halved

2 **eggs**

½ cup **matzo meal** or finely crushed unsalted soda crackers

1½ tsp **salt**

½ tsp **pepper**

Vegetable oil for frying

By hand or in food processor with shredder blade, grate potatoes alternating with onions. In large bowl, whisk together eggs, matzo meal, salt and pepper. Add potatoes and onions; toss to combine.

Pour enough oil into each of 2 large heavy skillets to come ¼ inch (5 mm) up sides; heat over medium-high heat until hot but not smoking. Using 2 tbsp lightly packed potato mixture per latke, add to pan, leaving 1 inch (2.5 cm) between each; flatten slightly. Fry, turning once, until edges are golden and crisp, about 5 minutes. Drain on paper towel–lined racks.

With small sieve, remove any potato pieces from oil and discard. Repeat with remaining latke mixture, heating more oil as necessary. *(Make-ahead: Let cool. Cover and refrigerate on paper towel–lined rimmed baking sheet for up to 8 hours. Recrisp on unlined baking sheets in 450°F/230°C oven for about 5 minutes.)*

87

Makes about 72 pieces. PER PIECE: about 66 cal, 1 g pro, 5 g total fat (1 g sat. fat), 6 g carb, 1 g fibre, 5 mg chol, 51 mg sodium. % RDI: 1% calcium, 1% iron, 1% vit A, 4% vit C, 2% folate.

Baked Potato Skins

Russets are fabulous baking potatoes. Use up the leftover cooked potato flesh from this recipe in hash browns the next morning or purée it into soups. Serve the crispy skins with sour cream for dipping.

9 **baking potatoes** (about 4 lb/1.8 kg)

1 tbsp **vegetable oil**

¼ tsp **salt**

8 slices **bacon,** cooked and crumbled

1½ cups shredded **old Cheddar cheese**

Pinch **cayenne pepper**

3 **green onions** (green parts only), thinly sliced

Scrub potatoes; pat dry. Prick several times with fork; rub with oil and sprinkle with salt. Bake in 425°F (220°C) oven until tender, about 1 hour. Let cool enough to handle. *(Make-ahead: Let cool completely. Refrigerate in airtight container for up to 24 hours.)*

Cut lengthwise in half; scoop out flesh, leaving ½-inch (1 cm) thick walls. Cut each half lengthwise in half; arrange, cut side up, on foil-lined rimmed baking sheet. Toss together bacon, Cheddar cheese and cayenne; sprinkle over potatoes. *(Make-ahead: Cover and refrigerate for up to 24 hours.)*

Bake in 425°F (220°C) oven until skins are crisp and cheese is melted, about 20 minutes. Transfer to platter. Sprinkle with green onions.

89

Change It Up

BAKED SWEET POTATO SKINS

Substitute sweet potatoes for potatoes and Swiss cheese for Cheddar. Top with dollop of plain yogurt before sprinkling with green onions.

Makes 36 pieces. PER PIECE: about 59 cal, 2 g pro, 3 g total fat (1 g sat. fat), 7 g carb, 1 g fibre, 6 mg chol, 71 mg sodium. % RDI: 4% calcium, 4% iron, 2% vit A, 5% vit C, 5% folate.

Blue Cheese & Walnut Mushrooms

Mushrooms are delicious partners for rich, cheesy fillings. Look for uniformly sized mushrooms that are about 2 inches (5 cm) across. For a pretty finish, top each with a tiny sprinkle of herbs, such as thyme, chives or parsley.

24 **mushrooms** (about 1 lb/450 g)

1 tbsp **vegetable oil**

STUFFING:

4 oz (115 g) **blue cheese,** at room temperature

½ cup chopped **walnuts**

½ cup **sour cream**

¼ tsp **pepper**

Remove stems from mushrooms; place caps, hollow side down, on foil-lined rimmed baking sheet. Brush with oil. Bake in 400°F (200°C) oven until slightly softened, about 8 minutes. Let cool; drain off liquid. Place, hollow side up, on clean foil-lined rimmed baking sheet.

STUFFING: In bowl, mash together blue cheese, walnuts, sour cream and pepper. Spoon into mushroom caps. Bake in 375°F (190°C) oven until golden, about 12 minutes.

Change It Up

GOAT CHEESE & SUN-DRIED TOMATO MUSHROOMS

Omit Stuffing. Substitute 5 oz (140 g) soft goat cheese, half pkg (250 g pkg) cream cheese, ⅓ cup chopped rinsed drained oil-packed sun-dried tomatoes, 2 tbsp chopped fresh parsley, 1 tbsp lemon juice and ¼ tsp pepper.

CREAMY GREMOLATA MUSHROOMS

Omit Stuffing. Substitute half pkg (250 g pkg) cream cheese; 1 cup chopped fresh parsley; 2 tbsp extra-virgin olive oil; 3 cloves garlic, minced; 1 tbsp grated lemon zest; and pinch each salt and pepper.

PROSCIUTTO & CHEDDAR MUSHROOMS

Omit Stuffing. Substitute half pkg (250 g pkg) cream cheese; 1 cup shredded Cheddar cheese; ¼ cup sour cream; 2 oz (55 g) prosciutto, diced; and ¼ tsp pepper.

BOURSIN & GREEN ONION MUSHROOMS

Omit Stuffing. Substitute 1 pkg (113 g) Herb and Garlic Boursin cheese; ¼ cup sour cream; and 2 green onions, minced.

Makes 24 pieces. PER PIECE: about 48 cal, 2 g pro, 4 g total fat (2 g sat. fat), 1 g carb, trace fibre, 5 mg chol, 68 mg sodium. % RDI: 3% calcium, 2% iron, 2% vit A, 3% folate.

90

From left: Blue Cheese & Walnut Mushrooms,
Goat Cheese & Sun-Dried Tomato Mushrooms
and Creamy Gremolata Mushrooms

CHAPTER 4

SAVOURY
pastries

From top: Ham & Gruyère Pinwheels (page 102) and Olive, Pepper & Asiago Pinwheels (page 104)

93

Aged Cheddar & Bacon Tartlets

Five-year-old Cheddar will give these morsels the most flavour; if you like a slightly milder taste, go with a three-year-old Cheddar. If you're out of 18% cream, substitute ⅔ cup each whipping cream (35%) and milk.

2 **eggs**

1⅓ cups **18% cream**

¼ tsp **salt**

Pinch each **pepper** and **nutmeg**

8 slices **bacon,** cooked until crisp and diced

⅓ cup thinly sliced **green onions**

1½ cups shredded **3- to 5-year-old Cheddar cheese** (6 oz/170 g)

TARTLET SHELLS:

½ cup cold **unsalted butter,** cubed

1 tbsp cold **lard,** shortening or butter, cubed

1⅔ cups **all-purpose flour**

1 **egg yolk**

¼ cup **ice water**

TARTLET SHELLS: In food processor, pulse butter and lard into flour until in coarse crumbs. Pulse in egg yolk and water just until pastry holds together. (Or, in bowl, using pastry blender or 2 knives, cut butter and lard into flour until in coarse crumbs. Whisk egg yolk with water; drizzle over dry ingredients, stirring briskly with fork just until dough holds together.) Divide dough in half; press into 2 discs; wrap and refrigerate for 1 hour.

On lightly floured surface, roll out each disc to ⅛-inch (3 mm) thickness; cut out twelve 3½-inch (9 cm) rounds from each. Fit into twenty-four 2¼-inch (5.5 cm) greased muffin cups; refrigerate for 30 minutes.

Beat together eggs, cream, salt, pepper and nutmeg until combined but not frothy. Divide bacon and green onions among tartlet shells; fill loosely with Cheddar cheese, mounding in centre. Pour in egg mixture to rim of pastry.

Bake on bottom rack in 400°F (200°C) oven until lightly browned, about 20 minutes. Serve warm. *(Make-ahead: Let cool in pan on rack for 10 minutes. Transfer to rack; let cool completely. Refrigerate for up to 3 days; reheat on baking sheet in 400°F/ 200°C oven until hot, about 4 minutes.)*

94

Makes 24 pieces. PER PIECE: about 136 cal, 4 g pro, 10 g total fat (6 g sat. fat), 7 g carb, trace fibre, 51 mg chol, 128 mg sodium, 54 mg potassium. % RDI: 6% calcium, 4% iron, 8% vit A, 10% folate.

Zucchini Sun-Dried Tomato Tartlets

These savoury quichelike tarts freeze and reheat exceptionally well. For a taste sensation, top the warm tartlets with a curl of aged Gouda cheese.

Half batch **Sour Cream Pastry**
(page 99)

1 tbsp **olive oil**

1 **shallot,** finely diced

1 clove **garlic,** minced

⅔ cup finely diced **zucchini**

3 tbsp diced drained **oil-packed sun-dried tomatoes**

½ tsp **dried oregano**

¼ tsp **salt**

¼ tsp **pepper**

¼ cup **10% cream**

1 **egg**

96

On lightly floured surface, roll out pastry to scant ⅛-inch (3 mm) thickness. Using 2¾-inch (7 cm) round cookie cutter, cut out 24 circles, rerolling scraps. Fit into ¾-inch (2 cm) deep mini-tart or mini-muffin cups. Prick all over with fork; freeze until firm, 20 minutes. Bake in 350°F (180°C) oven until light golden, 15 minutes. If dough puffs, gently press with fingertip. Let cool in pan on rack.

In skillet, heat oil over medium heat; cook shallot and garlic, stirring occasionally, until translucent, about 2 minutes. Add zucchini, tomatoes, oregano, and pinch each of the salt and pepper; cook, stirring, until zucchini is tender and golden, 5 to 7 minutes. Let cool. Divide among pastry shells.

Whisk together cream, egg and remaining salt and pepper; pour into shells, just to rim. Bake in 350°F (180°C) oven until knife inserted in centre comes out clean, 20 minutes. Let cool in pan on rack for 5 minutes. *(Make-ahead: Let cool for 30 minutes. Refrigerate in airtight container for up to 24 hours or freeze for up to 2 weeks. Reheat in 350°F/180°C oven for about 10 minutes, 15 minutes if frozen.)*

Makes 24 pieces. PER PIECE: about 75 cal, 1 g pro, 5 g total fat (3 g sat. fat), 6 g carb, trace fibre, 16 mg chol, 68 mg sodium, 37 mg potassium. % RDI: 1% calcium, 3% iron, 3% vit A, 2% vit C, 7% folate.

Mushroom Crescents

Cream cheese makes this pastry wonderfully tender – the perfect partner for two types of mushrooms accented with herbs.

2 tbsp **butter**

1 small **onion,** chopped

3 cloves **garlic,** minced

¾ tsp each **dried thyme** and **dried sage**

½ tsp **pepper**

¼ tsp **salt**

1½ cups finely chopped **portobello mushrooms**

1½ cups finely chopped **button mushrooms**

⅓ cup **white wine** or water

PASTRY:

½ cup **cream cheese,** softened

⅓ cup **butter,** softened

1 cup **all-purpose flour**

1 **egg,** beaten

In large saucepan, melt butter over medium heat; cook onion, garlic, thyme, sage, pepper and salt, stirring occasionally, until onion is softened, about 3 minutes.

Add portobello and button mushrooms; cook over medium-high heat, stirring occasionally, until browned, about 10 minutes. Stir in wine, scraping up browned bits from bottom of pan. Cook until no liquid remains, about 5 minutes. Let cool to room temperature. *(Make-ahead: Refrigerate in airtight container for up to 24 hours.)*

PASTRY: In large bowl, beat cream cheese with butter until fluffy. Stir in flour until dough begins to form; knead in bowl until smooth. Divide in half; flatten into discs. Wrap in plastic wrap; refrigerate until firm, about 30 minutes. *(Make-ahead: Refrigerate for up to 2 days.)*

On lightly floured surface, roll out each disc into 10-inch (25 cm) circle. With 2½-inch (6 cm) round cookie cutter, cut out circles, rerolling scraps once.

Working with 6 circles at a time, brush edges lightly with egg. Place 1 tsp filling in centre of each; fold dough over filling, pinching edges to seal. Place on ungreased rimmed baking sheet. Brush tops with remaining egg. *(Make-ahead: Layer between waxed paper and freeze in airtight container for up to 3 weeks. Bake from frozen.)*

Bake in 400°F (200°C) oven until light golden, 12 to 15 minutes. Serve warm or at room temperature.

97

Makes about 40 pieces. PER PIECE: about 45 cal, 1 g pro, 3 g total fat (2 g sat. fat), 3 g carb, trace fibre, 14 mg chol, 46 mg sodium. % RDI: 1% calcium, 2% iron, 4% vit A, 1% folate.

From top: Mini
Smoked Salmon
Dill Quiches
(opposite) and
Western-Style
Devilled Eggs
(page 190)

Mini Smoked Salmon Dill Quiches

These small, smoky morsels are a cocktail party staple. The sour cream pastry is a classic recipe, suited to all sorts of pies and savouries.

Sour Cream Pastry (below)

FILLING:

6 oz (170 g) **smoked salmon,** chopped

Half pkg (250 g pkg) **cream cheese,** diced

4 **eggs**

1 cup **milk**

2½ tbsp chopped **fresh dill**

2 **green onions,** minced

¼ tsp each **salt** and **pepper**

On lightly floured surface, roll out pastry to generous ⅛-inch (3 mm) thickness. Using 4-inch (10 cm) round pastry cutter, cut out 24 rounds. Fit into 24 muffin cups, without trimming. Prick all over with fork. Place on large rimmed baking sheet; refrigerate for 30 minutes.

Line shells with foil; fill with pie weights or dried beans. Bake on bottom rack in 400°F (200°C) oven until rims are light golden, about 10 minutes. Remove weights and foil; let cool in pan on rack.

FILLING: Sprinkle salmon and cream cheese in shells. Whisk together eggs, milk, dill, green onions, salt and pepper; pour into shells.

Bake in 375°F (190°C) oven until knife inserted in centre comes out clean, about 20 minutes. Let cool in pan on rack for 5 minutes. *(Make-ahead: Let cool. Layer between waxed paper in airtight container and refrigerate for up to 24 hours or freeze for up to 2 weeks. Thaw if frozen; reheat in 350°F/180°C oven for 10 minutes.)*

99

Make Your Own

SOUR CREAM PASTRY

In bowl, whisk 2½ cups all-purpose flour with ½ tsp salt. Using pastry blender, cut in ½ cup each cold butter and cold lard, cubed, until mixture resembles fine crumbs with a few larger pieces. Whisk ¼ cup ice water with 3 tbsp sour cream; drizzle over dry ingredients, stirring briskly with fork until ragged dough forms. Divide in half; press into discs. Wrap each in plastic wrap; refrigerate until chilled, about 30 minutes. *(Make-ahead: Refrigerate for up to 3 days.)*
Makes enough for 24 mini-quiches, or 1 double-crust 9-inch (23 cm) pie.

Makes 24 pieces. PER PIECE: about 151 cal, 4 g pro, 11 g total fat (5 g sat. fat), 9 g carb, trace fibre, 52 mg chol, 177 mg sodium, 63 mg potassium. % RDI: 2% calcium, 6% iron, 7% vit A, 13% folate.

Lamb Sausage Rolls

Guests will love the orange and fennel flavours of these two-bite rolls. If you're not a lamb fan, the ground beef alternative is very tasty, too.

2 **eggs**

¼ cup **fresh bread crumbs,** toasted

¼ cup minced **onion**

1 clove **garlic,** minced

2 tbsp chopped **fresh parsley**

2 tsp crushed **fennel seeds**

1 tsp grated **orange zest**

½ tsp each **salt** and **ground coriander**

¼ tsp **pepper**

1 lb (450 g) **ground lamb** or lean ground beef

Quick Puff Pastry (page 108) or 1 pkg (450 g) frozen butter puff pastry, thawed

2 tbsp **Dijon mustard**

1 **egg yolk**

In large bowl, stir together eggs, bread crumbs, onion, garlic, parsley, fennel seeds, orange zest, salt, coriander and pepper; mix in lamb. Set aside.

Divide pastry in half. On lightly floured surface, roll out each half into 10-inch (25 cm) square; cut each into 3 equal strips. Brush with mustard. Evenly spoon filling down centre of each strip. Fold pastry over filling to enclose; pinch seams to seal.

Arrange rolls, seam side down, on parchment paper–lined rimmed baking sheet. Cover and chill until firm, about 25 minutes. On cutting board and using serrated knife, cut each roll into 10 pieces; return pieces to pan. *(Make-ahead: Layer between waxed paper in airtight container and freeze for up to 2 weeks. Bake from frozen, increasing baking time by 5 minutes.)*

Whisk egg yolk with 1 tbsp water; brush over rolls. Bake in 450°F (230°C) oven until puffed and golden, about 20 minutes.

100

Makes 60 pieces. PER PIECE: about 66 cal, 2 g pro, 5 g total fat (3 g sat. fat), 3 g carb, trace fibre, 23 mg chol, 63 mg sodium. % RDI: 1% calcium, 3% iron, 3% vit A, 5% folate.

Tourtière Turnovers

A Canadian holiday tradition gets a cocktail party makeover. Serve these tender bites with old-fashioned tomato-based chili sauce.

⅔ cup cubed peeled **potato**

12 oz (340 g) **lean ground pork**

1 small **onion,** finely chopped

2 cloves **garlic,** minced

1 rib **celery,** finely chopped

1 cup diced **mushrooms**

½ cup **sodium-reduced chicken broth**

¾ tsp **salt**

½ tsp each **pepper** and **dried thyme**

¼ tsp each **ground cloves** and **cinnamon**

1 **bay leaf**

1 **egg yolk**

PASTRY:

3 cups **all-purpose flour**

1 tsp **salt**

½ cup each cold **butter** and **lard,** cubed

1 **egg**

2 tsp **vinegar** or lemon juice

Ice water

PASTRY: In bowl, whisk flour with salt. Using pastry blender, cut in butter and lard until in fine crumbs with a few larger pieces. In liquid measure, whisk egg with vinegar; add enough ice water to make ⅔ cup. Drizzle over dry ingredients, stirring with fork until ragged dough forms. Divide in half; press into discs. Wrap; refrigerate until chilled, 30 minutes. *(Make-ahead: Refrigerate for up to 3 days.)*

Cover and microwave potato with 2 tbsp water on high until tender, 5 minutes. Drain; mash. In skillet, cook pork over medium-high heat, breaking up, until no longer pink, 6 minutes. Drain off fat. Add onion, garlic, celery, mushrooms, broth, salt, pepper, thyme, cloves, cinnamon and bay leaf; bring to boil. Reduce heat, cover and simmer for 10 minutes. Uncover; cook until no liquid remains, 5 minutes. Discard bay leaf. Stir in potato. Let cool.

Divide pastry in half. On floured surface, roll out to scant ¼-inch (5 mm) thickness. Using 3-inch (8 cm) round cutter, cut out circles, rerolling scraps. Place scant 1 tbsp filling in centre of each. Brush edge with water; fold pastry over to create half-moon; seal edge with fork. Place on parchment paper–lined rimmed baking sheets. *(Make-ahead: Freeze until firm. Layer between waxed paper in airtight container and freeze for up to 2 weeks. Reheat from frozen, adding 5 minutes to baking time.)*

Whisk egg yolk with 1 tbsp water; brush over pastry. Cut steam vents in centres. Bake on bottom rack in 425°F (220°C) oven for 15 minutes. Reduce heat to 350°F (180°C); bake until golden, 15 minutes.

101

Makes about 40 pieces. PER PIECE: about 95 cal, 3 g pro, 6 g total fat (3 g sat. fat), 7 g carb, trace fibre, 25 mg chol, 130 mg sodium. % RDI: 1% calcium, 4% iron, 2% vit A, 9% folate.

Ham & Gruyère Pinwheels

Buttery pastry swirls rolled around savoury fillings are mouthwatering – and attractive. Make an assortment to freeze and enjoy over and over.

1 pkg (397 g) **frozen puff pastry,** thawed

1 **egg**

FILLING:

½ cup **mango chutney,** strained

4 oz (115 g) thinly sliced **Black Forest ham**

½ cup shredded **Gruyère cheese**

On lightly floured surface, roll out half of the pastry into 12-inch (30 cm) square.

FILLING: Leaving ½-inch (1 cm) border, spread half of the mango chutney over pastry. Arrange half of the ham in single layer over top; top with half of the cheese.

Whisk egg with 1 tbsp water; brush lightly over border. Roll up firmly into cylinder; pinch seam to seal. Repeat with remaining pastry, filling and egg mixture. Wrap in plastic wrap; refrigerate until firm, about 1 hour. *(Make-ahead: Refrigerate for up to 24 hours.)*

Using serrated knife, cut into scant ½-inch (1 cm) thick slices. Arrange, cut side down, on rimless baking sheets. *(Make-ahead: Freeze until firm; layer between waxed paper in airtight container and freeze for up to 2 weeks. Bake from frozen.)*

Bake in 425°F (220°C) oven until golden, about 15 minutes.

Change It Up

PROSCIUTTO & SAGE PINWHEELS

Omit Filling. Spread each half of pastry with 2 tbsp sweet mustard. Sprinkle each with 1 tbsp chopped fresh sage (or 1 tsp crumbled dried). Top each with 6 thin slices prosciutto in single layer.

STILTON & WALNUT PINWHEELS

Omit Filling. Combine 1 cup crumbled Stilton cheese, ¼ cup finely chopped toasted walnuts and ½ tsp pepper. Sprinkle half over each half of pastry.

102

Makes about 30 pieces. PER PIECE: about 97 cal, 2 g pro, 6 g total fat (1 g sat. fat), 8 g carb, trace fibre, 10 mg chol, 186 mg sodium. % RDI: 2% calcium, 3% iron, 1% vit A, 3% folate.

From top: Ham & Gruyère Pinwheels
(opposite) and Olive, Pepper & Asiago
Pinwheels (page 104)

Olive, Pepper & Asiago Pinwheels

Frozen puff pastry is convenient to have on hand for last-minute or freeze-ahead appetizers. Here, it encloses a tasty swirl of black olives, red peppers and Asiago cheese.

1 pkg (397 g) **frozen puff pastry,** thawed

½ cup shredded **Asiago cheese**

¼ cup finely chopped drained **jarred roasted red pepper**

¼ cup finely chopped **black olives**

1 tbsp chopped **fresh parsley**

½ tsp **dried oregano**

¼ tsp each **salt** and **pepper**

2 tbsp **Dijon mustard**

On lightly floured surface, roll out half of the pastry into 12-inch (30 cm) square.

In bowl, combine Asiago cheese, red pepper, olives, parsley, oregano, salt and pepper.

Spread half of the mustard over pastry. Leaving ½-inch (1 cm) border, sprinkle evenly with half of the cheese mixture. Roll up firmly into cylinder; pinch seam to seal.

Using serrated knife, cut into ½-inch (1 cm) thick slices. Arrange, cut side down, on rimless baking sheet. Repeat with remaining pastry, mustard and cheese mixture. *(Make-ahead: Freeze until firm; layer between waxed paper in airtight container and freeze for up to 2 weeks. Bake from frozen.)*

Bake in 425°F (220°C) oven until golden, about 15 minutes.

104

How-To

FREEZING UNCUT ROLLS AHEAD

Wrap uncut rolls in plastic wrap, overwrap with heavy-duty foil and freeze for up to 2 weeks. Thaw in refrigerator for 30 minutes, then slice and bake as directed.

Makes about 40 pieces. PER PIECE: about 62 cal, 1 g pro, 4 g total fat (1 g sat. fat), 5 g carb, trace fibre, 1 mg chol, 67 mg sodium. % RDI: 1% calcium, 2% iron, 1% vit A, 3% vit C, 2% folate.

Golden Chicken, Brie & Cranberry Turnovers

Golden puffed triangles of pastry are an easy and appetizing way to wrap up leftover chicken or turkey.

1 pkg (450 g) **frozen butter puff pastry,** thawed, or Quick Puff Pastry (page 108)

1 **egg,** beaten

FILLING:

1¼ cups diced **cooked chicken** or turkey

½ cup diced **Brie cheese**

1 **green onion,** finely chopped

1 clove **garlic,** minced

2 tbsp **light mayonnaise**

1 tbsp finely chopped **fresh sage** (or 1 tsp dried)

¼ tsp each **salt** and **pepper**

⅓ cup chopped **fresh cranberries**

FILLING: In bowl, combine chicken, Brie cheese, green onion, garlic, mayonnaise, sage, salt and pepper; stir in cranberries just until combined.

Unroll pastry; roll out each sheet into 10-inch (25 cm) squares if necessary. Cut into 16 squares each; brush edges lightly with some of the egg. Place heaping 1 tsp filling in centre of each; fold over to form triangle, pressing edges to seal.

Place on parchment paper–lined rimmed baking sheets; brush tops with remaining egg. *(Make-ahead: Cover and refrigerate for up to 4 hours. Or freeze until firm; layer between waxed paper in airtight container and freeze for up to 1 month. Bake from frozen, adding 3 minutes to baking time.)*

Bake in top and bottom thirds of 375°F (190°C) oven, rotating and switching pans halfway through, until golden and puffed, 20 minutes.

105

Makes 32 pieces. PER PIECE: about 84 cal, 3 g pro, 5 g total fat (2 g sat. fat), 6 g carb, trace fibre, 20 mg chol, 98 mg sodium. % RDI: 1% calcium, 4% iron, 3% vit A, 2% folate.

From left: Shrimp & Tarragon Puffs (opposite) and Welly Bites (page 108)

Shrimp & Tarragon Puffs

It doesn't matter what size shrimp you use in these pastries; just make sure they're raw – not cooked – so that they don't overcook when baked.

1 tbsp **butter**

¾ cup thinly sliced **leeks** (white and light green parts only) or finely diced onion

1 tbsp **all-purpose flour**

1 tbsp **tomato paste**

½ tsp **sweet paprika**

¼ tsp each **salt** and **pepper**

¼ cup **whipping cream** (35%)

2 tbsp **dry white wine** or vegetable broth

1 pkg (450 g) **frozen butter puff pastry,** thawed, or Quick Puff Pastry (page 108)

8 oz (225 g) **raw shrimp,** peeled and deveined

1 tbsp chopped **fresh tarragon** or parsley

1 **egg**

In saucepan, melt butter over medium heat; cook leeks, stirring, until softened, about 5 minutes. Stir in flour; cook, stirring, for 1 minute. Stir in tomato paste, all but pinch of the paprika, the salt and pepper; cook for 1 minute.

Whisk in cream and wine; bring to boil. Reduce heat and simmer until thickened, about 3 minutes. Let cool for 30 minutes, stirring occasionally. *(Make-ahead: Refrigerate in airtight container for up to 8 hours.)*

On floured surface, roll out 1 sheet of the pastry to 12-inch (30 cm) square. Using 3½-inch (9 cm) fluted round cutter, cut out 14 rounds, rerolling scraps.

Stir shrimp and tarragon into filling. Place scant 1 tbsp filling in centre of each round. Brush edge with water; fold pastry over to create half-moon, pressing edges to seal. Place on parchment paper–lined or greased rimmed baking sheet. Prick each puff once with fork; refrigerate for 30 minutes. Repeat with remaining pastry and filling. *(Make-ahead: Cover and refrigerate for up to 8 hours. Or freeze until firm; layer between waxed paper in airtight container and freeze for up to 2 weeks. Bake from frozen, adding 3 minutes to baking time.)*

Beat together egg, 2 tsp water and remaining paprika; brush over puffs. Bake in 425°F (220°C) oven until puffed and golden, about 15 minutes. Serve warm.

107

Makes 28 pieces. PER PIECE: about 108 cal, 2 g pro, 8 g total fat (5 g sat. fat), 6 g carb, trace fibre, 37 mg chol, 99 mg sodium. % RDI: 1% calcium, 4% iron, 8% vit A, 8% folate.

Welly Bites

Inspired by classic Beef Wellington, which had its heyday in the 1960s, this finger-food version requires fewer steps and ingredients but delivers just as much flavour.

3 tbsp **Dijon mustard**

1 tbsp chopped **fresh thyme** (or 1 tsp dried)

¼ tsp each **salt** and **pepper**

12 oz (340 g) **beef tenderloin premium oven roast,** cut in 1-inch (2.5 cm) cubes

1 pkg (450 g) **frozen butter puff pastry,** thawed, or Quick Puff Pastry (below)

1 **egg**

In bowl, stir together mustard, thyme, salt and pepper; add beef, tossing to coat.

On lightly floured surface, roll out 1 sheet of the pastry into 12-inch (30 cm) square; cut into 16 squares. Repeat with remaining pastry.

Place 1 piece mustard-coated beef in centre of each square. Brush edges of pastry with water. Bring up corners and pinch together in centre; pinch sides closed. Transfer to parchment paper–lined or greased rimmed baking sheet; refrigerate for 30 minutes. *(Make-ahead: Cover and refrigerate for up to 12 hours.)*

Beat egg with 2 tsp water; brush over pastry. Bake in 425°F (220°C) oven until golden and puffed, about 15 minutes. Serve warm.

Make Your Own

QUICK PUFF PASTRY

Cut 1 cup cold unsalted butter into ½-inch (1 cm) cubes; set aside ¾ cup in refrigerator. In food processor, blend 1⅔ cups all-purpose flour with ¾ tsp salt. Sprinkle remaining butter over top; pulse until indistinguishable, 10 seconds. Sprinkle with reserved butter; pulse 4 or 5 times until in pea-size pieces. Drizzle ⅓ cup cold water evenly over mixture (not through feed tube). Pulse 6 to 8 times until loose ragged dough forms (do not let form ball). Transfer to floured waxed paper; press into rectangle. Dust with flour; top with waxed paper. Roll out into 15- x 12-inch (38 x 30 cm) rectangle. Remove top paper. Starting at long edge and using bottom paper to lift pastry, fold over one-third; fold opposite long edge over top, bringing flush with edge of first fold to make 15- x 4-inch (38 x 10 cm) rectangle. Starting from 1 short end, roll up firmly; flatten into 5-inch (12 cm) square. Cut in half; wrap and refrigerate until firm, 1 hour. *(Make-ahead: Refrigerate for up to 5 days or freeze in airtight container for up to 2 weeks.)* **Makes 1 lb (450 g).**

Makes 32 pieces. PER PIECE: about 95 cal, 3 g pro, 7 g total fat (4 g sat. fat), 5 g carb, trace fibre, 27 mg chol, 99 mg sodium. % RDI: 1% calcium, 5% iron, 6% vit A, 7% folate.

108

Cheeseburger Spring Rolls

The crunchy double wrappers on these East-meets-West bites keep the filling snug inside. Processed cheese may seem odd, but it gives the rolls an iconic cheeseburger taste, especially when dipped in ketchup and mustard.

1 tsp **olive oil**

1 cup diced **red onion**

2 cloves **garlic,** minced

8 oz (225 g) **lean ground beef**

1 cup cubed **processed cheese product** (such as Velveeta)

1 cup **fresh bread crumbs**

¼ cup diced **dill pickle,** patted dry

2 **green onions,** chopped

1 tbsp **mustard**

1 tsp **Worcestershire sauce**

½ tsp **pepper**

1 **egg**

64 **spring roll wrappers**

In skillet, heat oil over medium heat; cook red onion and garlic, stirring occasionally, until softened, about 5 minutes.

Add beef; cook, breaking up with spoon, until no longer pink, about 4 minutes. Drain in sieve, pressing out liquid. Return to pan. Stir in cheese; cook over medium heat until melted, about 2 minutes. Scrape into bowl.

Stir in bread crumbs, dill pickle, green onions, mustard, Worcestershire sauce and pepper; let cool for 15 minutes.

Mix egg with 2 tsp water. Layer 2 spring roll wrappers on work surface with 1 corner facing up; place 1 tbsp beef mixture on bottom third of wrapper. Fold bottom corner of wrapper over filling; fold in sides and roll up until 2-inch (5 cm) triangle of wrapper remains at top. Lightly brush some of the egg mixture over triangle and loosely roll up to seal. Repeat with remaining filling, wrappers and egg mixture.

Place rolls, seam side down, on parchment paper–lined rimmed baking sheet. *(Make-ahead: Cover and refrigerate for up to 12 hours; bake as directed. Or freeze on baking sheet for 1 hour; transfer to airtight container and freeze for up to 2 weeks. Bake in 350°F/180°C oven for 30 minutes.)*

Bake in 375°F (190°C) oven, turning once, until light golden, about 25 minutes. Serve warm.

109

Makes 32 pieces. PER PIECE: about 124 cal, 5 g pro, 3 g total fat (2 g sat. fat), 18 g carb, trace fibre, 12 mg chol, 218 mg sodium, 36 mg potassium. % RDI: 2% calcium, 1% iron, 1% vit A, 1% folate.

Roasted Cherry Tomato Tart

Goat cheese, olives and roasted tomatoes add up to delicious, intense flavour. The tender, slightly crunchy cornmeal pastry is supple and easy to work with.

4 cups **cherry tomatoes** or grape tomatoes

4 tsp **extra-virgin olive oil**

1 clove **garlic,** minced

¼ tsp each **salt** and **pepper**

1 tbsp **Dijon mustard**

½ cup crumbled **soft goat cheese**

8 **brine-cured black olives** (such as Kalamata), quartered lengthwise

CORNMEAL PASTRY:

1 cup **all-purpose flour**

½ cup **cornmeal**

2 tsp chopped **fresh thyme** (or ½ tsp dried)

½ tsp **salt**

½ cup cold **butter,** diced

3 tbsp **ice water**

2 tsp **lemon juice** or vinegar

Change It Up

ROASTED CHERRY TOMATO TARTLETS

Divide dough into sixths; roll into 5½-inch (13 cm) rounds. Fit into 4-inch (10 cm) tart pans with removable bottoms. Reduce shell and tartlet baking times by about 2 minutes each. **Makes 6 tartlets.**

CORNMEAL PASTRY: In food processor, blend together flour, cornmeal, thyme and salt; pulse in butter until mixture resembles fine crumbs with a few larger pieces. With motor running, add ice water and lemon juice all at once; pulse just until dough starts to clump together. Remove and press into disc. Wrap and refrigerate until chilled, about 30 minutes. *(Make-ahead: Refrigerate for up to 2 days. Let come to room temperature.)*

On floured surface, roll out dough into 11-inch (28 cm) circle. Drape over 9-inch (23 cm) tart pan with removable bottom. Ease into pan without stretching; press over bottom and up side, folding in edge to make even with rim. Prick all over with fork. Refrigerate for 30 minutes. *(Make-ahead: Cover and refrigerate for up to 24 hours.)* Bake on bottom rack in 400°F (200°C) oven until golden, 18 to 20 minutes. Let cool in pan on rack.

Meanwhile, in 13- x 9-inch (3.5 L) metal cake pan, toss together cherry tomatoes, oil, garlic, salt and pepper. Roast in 400°F (200°C) oven until lightly charred and shrivelled, about 30 minutes. Let cool in pan. *(Make-ahead: Refrigerate in airtight container for up to 24 hours.)*

Brush bottom of tart shell with mustard; sprinkle with all but 2 tbsp of the goat cheese. Arrange tomato mixture over top; dot with olives and sprinkle with remaining goat cheese.

Bake in 400°F (200°C) oven until tomatoes are warmed through, about 14 minutes. Serve warm or at room temperature.

Makes 6 to 8 servings. PER EACH OF 8 SERVINGS: about 260 cal, 5 g pro, 17 g total fat (9 g sat. fat), 22 g carb, 2 g fibre, 35 mg chol, 440 mg sodium. % RDI: 3% calcium, 10% iron, 19% vit A, 17% vit C, 26% folate.

Gouda Bacon Puffs

These profiteroles with a twist are so addictive. This recipe can easily be halved to make fewer puffs, but they freeze so nicely that you might as well make the whole batch to keep on hand for impromptu guests.

½ cup **butter**

Pinch **salt**

1¼ cups **all-purpose flour**

4 **eggs**

1 cup shredded **Gouda cheese**

¼ cup crumbled **cooked bacon** (about 5 slices)

½ tsp chopped **fresh thyme**

112

In small heavy saucepan, bring 1 cup water, butter and salt to boil. Remove from heat. Add flour all at once, stirring vigorously with wooden spoon until mixture forms smooth ball that pulls away from side of pan. Return to medium-low heat; cook, stirring constantly, for 2 minutes. Let cool for 5 minutes.

Using wooden spoon, vigorously beat in eggs, 1 at a time, beating well after each addition; beat until smooth and shiny. Beat in cheese, bacon and thyme.

Spoon dough into pastry bag fitted with ½-inch (1 cm) round tip or resealable plastic bag with corner snipped off; pipe mounds, 1 inch (2.5 cm) in diameter and about 1 inch (2.5 cm) apart, onto greased or parchment paper–lined baking sheets. Using wet fingertip, gently flatten peak of each mound.

Bake, 1 sheet at a time, in 400°F (200°C) oven until puffed, golden and crisp, about 16 minutes. *(Make-ahead: Let cool. Store in airtight container for up to 2 days. Or freeze for up to 1 month; thaw and reheat in 350°F/180°C oven until hot, about 5 minutes.)*

Makes about 62 pieces. PER PIECE: about 36 cal, 1 g pro, 3 g total fat (1 g sat. fat), 2 g carb, trace fibre, 19 mg chol, 41 mg sodium, 12 mg potassium. % RDI: 1% calcium, 1% iron, 2% vit A, 3% folate.

Asparagus Provolone Toast Cups

Bite-size toast cups are no-fail containers for any kind of filling. They're perfect for parties: easier to make – and eat – than pastry.

5 stalks **asparagus,** trimmed

24 **Toast Cups** (page 131)

1 tbsp **Dijon mustard**

¾ cup shredded **provolone cheese**

Cut asparagus stalks into ¼-inch (5 mm) thick rounds; set aside.

Place toast cups in 1½-inch (4 cm) tart tins; brush with mustard. Mound cheese in cups; top each with 3 asparagus rounds. *(Make-ahead: Cover and refrigerate for up to 24 hours or layer between waxed paper in airtight container and freeze for up to 2 weeks. Bake from frozen.)*

Bake in 350°F (180°C) oven until cheese is melted, 15 to 20 minutes.

113

Change It Up

ASPARAGUS MOZZARELLA TOAST CUPS

Substitute mozzarella or any other semisoft or firm stretchy cheese – such as Gouda, Edam or Swiss – for the provolone.

Makes 24 pieces. PER PIECE: about 29 cal, 1 g pro, 2 g total fat (1 g sat. fat), 2 g carb, trace fibre, 2 mg chol, 63 mg sodium. % RDI: 3% calcium, 1% iron, 1% vit A, 4% folate.

From left: Tourtière Turnovers (page 101),
Lamb Sausage Rolls (page 100) and
Moroccan Chicken Triangles (opposite)

Moroccan Chicken Triangles

A blend of sweet and savoury North African spices is the flavour key to these flaky morsels. Browning the chicken makes it easier to dice.

6 sheets **phyllo pastry**

⅓ cup **butter,** melted

FILLING:

2 tbsp **vegetable oil**

1 lb (450 g) **boneless skinless chicken thighs**

1 **onion,** chopped

2 cloves **garlic,** minced

1 tsp each **ground ginger, sweet paprika** and **ground cumin**

½ tsp each **salt** and **cinnamon**

¼ tsp **pepper**

1 tbsp **tomato paste**

⅓ cup chopped **fresh cilantro**

¼ cup **slivered almonds**

FILLING: In large nonstick skillet, heat oil over medium-high heat; brown chicken, in batches. Transfer to plate and let cool enough to handle; dice. Drain fat from pan; fry chicken, onion, garlic, ginger, paprika, cumin, salt, cinnamon and pepper over medium heat, stirring often, until onion is softened, 5 minutes. Add ½ cup water and tomato paste; bring to boil. Reduce heat and simmer until almost no liquid remains, 6 minutes. Stir in cilantro and almonds. Let cool enough to handle.

Place 1 sheet of the phyllo on work surface, covering remainder with damp towel to prevent drying out. Brush lightly with some of the butter; cut lengthwise into 4 equal strips.

115

Spoon heaping 1 tbsp filling about ½ inch (1 cm) from end of each strip. Fold 1 corner of phyllo over filling so bottom edge meets side edge to form triangle; fold up triangle. Continue folding triangle sideways and upward to end of strip, without wrapping too tightly. Repeat with remaining phyllo and filling. Arrange on rimmed baking sheets. *(Make-ahead: Cover with plastic wrap; refrigerate for up to 24 hours. Or freeze until firm; layer between waxed paper in airtight container and freeze for up to 2 weeks. Bake from frozen, increasing baking time by 5 minutes.)*

Brush with remaining butter. Bake in 400°F (200°C) oven until golden, about 15 minutes.

Makes 24 pieces. PER PIECE: about 86 cal, 4 g pro, 6 g total fat (2 g sat. fat), 4 g carb, trace fibre, 24 mg chol, 121 mg sodium. % RDI: 1% calcium, 4% iron, 4% vit A, 2% vit C, 3% folate.

Phyllo Cups

For hors d'oeuvres, fill these crisp cups with a variety of savoury fillings (opposite). For desserts, fill them with ice cream and top with fruit or chocolate sauce. For best results, use ¾-inch (2 cm) deep muffin cups.

6 sheets **phyllo pastry**

¼ cup **butter,** melted

Place 1 sheet of the phyllo on work surface, covering remainder with damp towel to prevent drying out. Brush lightly with some of the butter. Top with 2 more phyllo sheets, brushing each with some of the remaining butter. Cut stack lengthwise into 4 strips and crosswise into 6 strips to make 24 squares.

Press squares into 24 greased mini-muffin cups or mini-tart tins. Bake in 400°F (200°C) oven until golden, about 5 minutes. Let cool in pan on rack. Repeat with remaining phyllo and butter. *(Make-ahead: Freeze in single layer in airtight container for up to 1 month. Recrisp in 350°F/180°C oven, about 3 minutes.)*

116

Makes 48 pieces. PER PIECE: about 18 cal, trace pro, 1 g total fat (1 g sat. fat), 2 g carb, 0 g fibre, 3 mg chol, 25 mg sodium. % RDI: 1% iron, 1% vit A, 1% folate.

ROAST BEEF & HORSERADISH PHYLLO CUPS

Blend together ⅔ cup spreadable cream cheese, 2 tbsp prepared horseradish, 1½ tsp grainy or Dijon mustard, and ½ tsp Worcestershire sauce. Cut 4-inch (10 cm) piece English cucumber into 48 thin slices; cut each in half. Trim any fat from 8 oz (225 g) shaved rare roast beef; cut into forty-eight 2- x 1½-inch (5 x 4 cm) pieces. Spoon cheese mixture into Phyllo Cups (opposite). Arrange 2 cucumber pieces on either side of each cup. Fold each beef slice in half lengthwise; crumple and fit into cup between cucumber slices.

Makes 48 pieces. PER PIECE: about 40 cal, 2 g pro, 3 g total fat (2 g sat. fat), 2 g carb, trace fibre, 11 mg chol, 46 mg sodium. % RDI: 1% iron, 2% vit A, 1% folate.

SMOKED SALMON PHYLLO CUPS

In bowl, mix together 1 pkg (250 g) cream cheese, softened; 6 oz (170 g) smoked salmon, chopped; 2 tbsp chopped fresh dill; and 1 tbsp lemon juice. Spoon into Phyllo Cups (opposite).

Makes 48 pieces. PER PIECE: about 39 cal, 1 g pro, 3 g total fat (2 g sat. fat), 2 g carb, 0 g fibre, 9 mg chol, 67 mg sodium. % RDI: 1% iron, 3% vit A, 1% folate.

CREAM CHEESE & HOT PEPPER JELLY PHYLLO CUPS

Mash 2 pkg (each 250 g) cream cheese, softened, with ¼ cup sour cream. Divide among Phyllo Cups (opposite). Garnish each with scant ¼ tsp hot pepper jelly.

Makes 48 pieces. PER PIECE: about 60 cal, 1 g pro, 5 g total fat (3 g sat. fat), 3 g carb, trace fibre, 15 mg chol, 56 mg sodium, 18 mg potassium. % RDI: 1% calcium, 1% iron, 5% vit A, 2% folate.

THAI CRAB SALAD PHYLLO CUPS

In bowl, whisk 3 tbsp lime juice; 3 tbsp vegetable oil; 2 tbsp granulated sugar; 2 tsp fish sauce; 1½ tsp peanut butter; 1 clove garlic, minced; and dash hot pepper sauce until sugar is dissolved. Squeeze any liquid from 8 oz (225 g) crabmeat (fresh or thawed). Add to bowl with ⅔ cup each finely chopped English cucumber and sweet red pepper; 3 tbsp finely chopped green onion; and 3 tbsp finely chopped fresh basil or mint. Toss; spoon into Phyllo Cups (opposite). Sprinkle with 2 tbsp finely chopped peanuts.

Makes 48 pieces. PER PIECE: about 37 cal, 2 g pro, 2 g total fat (1 g sat. fat), 3 g carb, trace fibre, 6 mg chol, 79 mg sodium. % RDI: 2% iron, 2% vit A, 8% vit C, 3% folate.

TOMATO GOAT CHEESE SALAD PHYLLO CUPS

In bowl, whisk 2 tbsp extra-virgin olive oil; 1 tbsp wine vinegar; 1 clove garlic, minced; 2 tsp chopped fresh thyme (or ¼ tsp dried); and ¼ tsp each salt and pepper. Add 2 cups cherry tomatoes, quartered; and 2 tbsp chopped fresh parsley. Spoon half tube (4½ oz/130 g tube) goat cheese, softened, into Phyllo Cups (opposite). Top with tomato mixture, and sliced olives (optional).

Makes 48 pieces. PER PIECE: about 27 cal, 1 g pro, 2 g total fat (1 g sat. fat), 2 g carb, trace fibre, 4 mg chol, 42 mg sodium. % RDI: 1% iron, 2% vit A, 2% vit C, 1% folate.

117

CURRIED CHICKEN SALAD PHYLLO CUPS

In bowl, stir together 2 boneless skinless chicken breasts, cooked and diced; 2 ribs celery, finely diced; 2 green onions, minced; ½ cup mayonnaise; 2 tsp lemon juice; 1 tsp mild curry paste; and ¼ tsp each salt and pepper. Spoon into Phyllo Cups (opposite). Top each with ¼ tsp mango chutney.

Makes 48 pieces. PER PIECE: about 42 cal, 2 g pro, 3 g total fat (1 g sat. fat), 2 g carb, trace fibre, 7 mg chol, 57 mg sodium, 26 mg potassium. % RDI: 1% iron, 1% vit A, 2% folate.

Feta Spinach Strudel Bites

For a milder taste, use Parmesan instead of the stronger Romano cheese.

9 sheets **phyllo pastry**

½ cup **butter,** melted

FILLING:

1 tbsp **vegetable oil**

1 **onion,** finely chopped

2 cloves **garlic,** minced

1 pkg (10 oz/300 g) **frozen spinach,** thawed

1 cup grated **Romano cheese**

1 cup crumbled **feta cheese**

1 **egg,** lightly beaten

¼ cup diced drained **jarred roasted red pepper**

3 tbsp chopped **fresh dill** (or 2 tsp dried dillweed)

½ tsp **pepper**

Pinch **nutmeg**

FILLING: In skillet, heat oil over medium heat; fry onion and garlic, stirring often, until softened, about 5 minutes. Scrape into bowl; let cool. Squeeze moisture from spinach; chop finely and add to bowl along with Romano and feta cheeses, egg, roasted red pepper, dill, pepper and nutmeg. Stir to combine.

Place 1 sheet of the phyllo on work surface, covering remainder with damp towel to prevent drying out. Brush lightly with some of the butter. Top with 2 more phyllo sheets, brushing each with some of the remaining butter.

Leaving 1-inch (2.5 cm) border on each end, spoon about 1 cup of the spinach mixture along 1 long side; fold ends over filling. Roll up to form log. Place, seam side down, on baking sheet. With sharp knife, score top through phyllo to make 12 servings. Repeat with remaining phyllo and filling and some of the remaining butter. *(Make-ahead: Cover with plastic wrap; refrigerate for up to 24 hours. Or freeze in airtight container for up to 2 weeks. Bake from frozen, increasing baking time by 5 minutes.)*

Brush with remaining butter. Bake in 400°F (200°C) oven until golden, about 25 minutes. With serrated knife, slice along score marks.

118

Makes 36 pieces. PER PIECE: about 69 cal, 2 g pro, 5 g total fat (3 g sat. fat), 4 g carb, trace fibre, 19 mg chol, 136 mg sodium. % RDI: 5% calcium, 3% iron, 8% vit A, 5% vit C, 6% folate.

Bacon, Onion & Goat Cheese Pizza Bites

If you prefer, you can use two 14-inch (35 cm) round pizza pans instead of the rectangular ones; the yield will be smaller and you won't have uniform squares. But they'll taste just as good!

5 cups **all-purpose flour** (approx)

2 cups **warm water**

2 tbsp **olive oil**

1 tbsp **liquid honey**

1 pkg (8 g) **active dry yeast** (or 2¼ tsp)

3 tbsp **sesame seeds**

1½ tsp **salt**

TOPPING:

6 oz (170 g) **thick-cut bacon,** diced (about 1⅓ cups)

2 cups thinly sliced **red onion**

1 bunch **green onions,** cut in 1-inch (2.5 cm) pieces

½ tsp **pepper**

⅔ cup grated **Romano cheese**

6 oz (170 g) **soft goat cheese,** crumbled (about 1¼ cups)

Stir together 1 cup of the flour, the warm water, oil, honey and yeast until combined. Cover with plastic wrap; let rise in warm, draft-free place until bubbly and almost doubled in bulk, about 1 hour.

With wooden spoon, stir in all but ½ cup of the remaining flour, sesame seeds and salt to form ragged dough. Turn out onto floured surface; knead, adding as much of the remaining flour as necessary to prevent sticking, until smooth and elastic, about 6 minutes.

Place in greased bowl, turning to grease all over. Cover with plastic wrap; let rise in warm, draft-free place until doubled in bulk, about 1½ hours.

Divide dough in half. Place each on greased 16- x 12-inch (40 x 30 cm) rimmed baking sheet. Pressing with fingertips and gently pulling at edges, stretch dough to fit pans.

TOPPING: Sprinkle bacon, red and green onions, and pepper evenly over dough; top with Romano cheese.

Bake on bottom rack in 450°F (230°C) oven until bottoms are golden, about 18 minutes. Sprinkle goat cheese over top; bake until goat cheese is slightly melted, about 4 minutes. Let cool for 5 minutes. Cut each pizza into 36 squares.

Makes 72 pieces. PER PIECE: about 61 cal, 2 g pro, 3 g total fat (1 g sat. fat), 8 g carb, trace fibre, 4 mg chol, 83 mg sodium, 27 mg potassium. % RDI: 2% calcium, 4% iron, 1% vit A, 10% folate.

120

Steak & Stilton Cheese in Toast Cups

To save time, you can substitute deli rare roast beef for the steak. For an extra pop of colour, cut 16 cherry tomatoes in half and broil alongside the steak; add to the toast cups with the steak.

2 tbsp **wine vinegar**

1 tbsp **olive oil**

2 cloves **garlic,** minced

¼ tsp **pepper**

8 oz (225 g) **top sirloin grilling steak,** 1 inch (2.5 cm) thick

⅓ cup **light mayonnaise**

1 tbsp **prepared horseradish**

32 **Toast Cups** (page 131)

4 oz (115 g) **Stilton cheese** (or other blue cheese), crumbled

In large shallow dish, stir together vinegar, oil, garlic and pepper. Add steak, turning to coat. Let stand at room temperature for 30 minutes.

Broil steak, turning once, until rare, about 7 minutes. Let cool. *(Make-ahead: Refrigerate in airtight container for up to 12 hours.)*

Slice steak very thinly; cut each slice in half. Stir mayonnaise with horseradish; spoon ½ tsp into bottom of each toast cup. Top with steak; sprinkle with about 1 tsp of the Stilton cheese.

121

Makes 32 pieces. PER PIECE: about 50 cal, 3 g pro, 3 g total fat (1 g sat. fat), 2 g carb, trace fibre, 8 mg chol, 76 mg sodium, 30 mg potassium. % RDI: 2% calcium, 2% iron, 2% vit A, 3% folate.

Chili Shrimp Wonton Cups

Using a juicy, ripe mango for this recipe ensures there's enough sweetness to complement the heat in the marinade. You'll usually find square wonton wrappers in the produce section of grocery stores.

25 **wonton wrappers**

2 tsp **olive oil**

½ cup diced pitted peeled **ripe mango**

2 tbsp **mayonnaise**

1 tbsp chopped **fresh cilantro**

2 tsp **lime juice**

1 tsp each **fish sauce** and **sesame oil**

3 tbsp **unsalted roasted peanuts,** chopped

CHILI SHRIMP:

2 tsp each **lime juice** and **sesame oil**

1 clove **garlic,** minced

Pinch **hot pepper flakes**

6 oz (170 g) **raw shrimp,** peeled and deveined

CHILI SHRIMP: In small bowl, stir together lime juice, sesame oil, garlic and hot pepper flakes; add shrimp, tossing to coat. Let stand for 20 minutes; drain well.

Meanwhile, lightly brush wonton wrappers with 1 tsp of the olive oil; press into mini-muffin cups. Bake in 400°F (200°C) oven until crisp and golden, about 6 minutes. *(Make-ahead: Store in airtight container for up to 1 week.)*

In skillet, heat remaining olive oil over medium-high heat; cook shrimp until pink, about 4 minutes. With slotted spoon, transfer to cutting board; chop into ¼-inch (5 mm) pieces.

Stir together shrimp, mango, mayonnaise, cilantro, lime juice, fish sauce and sesame oil. *(Make-ahead: Refrigerate in airtight container for up to 12 hours.)* Spoon into wonton cups; sprinkle with peanuts.

123

Change It Up

CHILI SHRIMP CUCUMBER ROUNDS

Omit wonton cups. Serve shrimp mixture on ¼-inch (5 mm) thick cucumber slices.

Makes 25 pieces. PER PIECE: about 53 cal, 2 g pro, 3 g total fat (trace sat. fat), 6 g carb, trace fibre, 9 mg chol, 78 mg sodium, 30 mg potassium. % RDI: 1% calcium, 3% iron, 1% vit A, 2% vit C, 4% folate.

Armenian Pizza Wedges

We've simplified these bites, traditionally made with pita dough, by using very similar prepared pizza dough.

8 oz (225 g) **lean ground lamb** or beef

⅓ cup finely chopped **fresh parsley**

¼ cup **butter,** melted

¼ cup **tomato paste**

1 **onion,** finely chopped

Half **sweet green pepper,** finely chopped

2 cloves **garlic,** minced

2 tsp **dried marjoram** or dried oregano

½ tsp each **ground allspice** and **salt**

¼ tsp each **cinnamon, pepper** and **cayenne pepper**

1 lb (450 g) **pizza dough**

Lemon wedges

Mix together lamb, parsley, butter, tomato paste, onion, green pepper, garlic, marjoram, allspice, salt, cinnamon, pepper and cayenne pepper; set aside.

Punch down dough; knead gently. Divide in half; roll each into wide log. Cut each log into 6 equal pieces; roll each into ball. Cover loosely with plastic wrap and let rest for 20 minutes.

On lightly floured surface, roll out balls into 5-inch (12 cm) circles; place on greased rimmed baking sheets. Divide meat mixture among circles, spreading to edges.

Bake in 450°F (230°C) oven until lightly browned, about 15 minutes. *(Make-ahead: Let cool. Layer between waxed paper in airtight container; refrigerate for up to 2 days or freeze for up to 2 weeks. Thaw in refrigerator; reheat in 400°F/ 200°C oven until hot but not dry, about 7 minutes.)*

Cut each circle into quarters; serve with lemon wedges to squeeze over top.

124

Makes 48 pieces. PER PIECE: about 45 cal, 2 g pro, 2 g total fat (1 g sat. fat), 5 g carb, trace fibre, 6 mg chol, 82 mg sodium. % RDI: 1% calcium, 3% iron, 2% vit A, 3% vit C, 2% folate.

Spicy Cheddar Shortbread

Chipotle chili and cheese give delicate shortbread a savoury makeover.

1 cup **butter,** softened

1 cup shredded **old Cheddar cheese**

¼ cup **cornstarch**

2 tbsp **granulated sugar**

1¾ cups **all-purpose flour**

½ tsp **chipotle chili powder** (or chili powder)

½ tsp **dry mustard**

¼ tsp each **salt** and **pepper**

In large bowl, beat butter until fluffy; beat in Cheddar cheese, cornstarch and sugar. Whisk together flour, chili powder, mustard, salt and pepper; stir into butter mixture. Shape dough into disc; wrap and refrigerate until firm, 30 minutes.

On lightly floured surface, roll out dough to ¼-inch (5 mm) thickness. Using 2-inch (5 cm) cookie cutter, cut out shapes, rerolling scraps. Arrange, 1 inch (2.5 cm) apart, on 2 parchment paper–lined rimless baking sheets. Chill until firm, about 30 minutes.

Bake in top and bottom thirds of 300°F (150°C) oven, rotating and switching pans halfway through, until shortbread are firm to the touch and light golden, about 20 minutes. Transfer to racks; let cool. *(Make-ahead: Layer between waxed paper in airtight container and store for up to 2 days or freeze for up to 1 month.)*

125

Change It Up

HERB & ASIAGO SHORTBREAD

Use Asiago cheese instead of Cheddar. Omit chili powder and mustard. Add ¾ tsp dried Italian herb seasoning.

Makes about 84 pieces. PER PIECE: about 37 cal, 1 g pro, 3 g total fat (2 g sat. fat), 3 g carb, 0 g fibre, 8 mg chol, 38 mg sodium. % RDI: 1% calcium, 1% iron, 3% vit A, 3% folate.

Curry Cashew Thumbprints

Thick, sweet, gingery Major Grey–style mango chutney is the tastiest choice for these savoury cookies.

¾ cup **unsalted butter,** softened

2 tbsp **granulated sugar**

1 tbsp **mild curry paste**

2 **eggs,** separated

1¾ cups **all-purpose flour**

¼ tsp **salt**

1 cup finely chopped **unsalted roasted cashews**

⅓ cup **mango chutney**

In bowl, beat together butter, sugar and curry paste until fluffy; beat in egg yolks, 1 at a time. Whisk flour with salt; stir into butter mixture.

In shallow bowl, whisk egg whites until frothy. Place cashews in separate bowl. Roll dough by scant 1 tbsp into balls; roll each in egg whites then in cashews to coat. Arrange, 2 inches (5 cm) apart, on parchment paper–lined or greased rimless baking sheets. Without cracking dough, gently press finger into centre of each to make well.

Bake in 325°F (160°C) oven until browned on bottoms, about 20 minutes. Let cool on pan on rack for 5 minutes, re-pressing wells if necessary. Transfer to racks; let cool. *(Make-ahead: Layer between waxed paper in airtight container and store for up to 5 days or freeze for up to 3 weeks.)*

Fill each well with some of the mango chutney.

Makes about 45 pieces. PER PIECE: about 82 cal, 2 g pro, 6 g total fat (2 g sat. fat), 7 g carb, trace fibre, 17 mg chol, 41 mg sodium. % RDI: 4% iron, 3% vit A, 6% folate.

Clockwise from top: Curry Cashew
Thumbprints (opposite), Olive
Pesto Biscotti (page 129) and Sage
Cornmeal Sticks (page 128)

Sage Cornmeal Sticks

Cornmeal gives cookies a pleasant crunch. The dough is soft and fairly easy to pipe, so it's a good recipe to try if you're new to piped cookies.

1 cup **butter,** softened

2 tbsp **liquid honey**

2 **eggs**

¼ cup **milk**

1½ cups each **all-purpose flour** and **cornmeal**

2 tsp chopped **fresh sage**

1 tsp **baking powder**

1 tsp **salt**

Refrigerate ungreased rimless baking sheets until chilled.

In large bowl, beat butter with honey until fluffy; beat in eggs and milk. Whisk together flour, cornmeal, sage, baking powder and salt; stir into butter mixture until smooth.

Spoon dough into piping bag fitted with large star tip; pipe into 3-inch (8 cm) long logs, about ½ inch (1 cm) apart, on chilled pans. Bake in 350°F (180°C) oven until slightly darker on bottoms, about 15 minutes.

Reduce temperature to 300°F (150°C); bake until crisp, about 15 minutes. Let cool on pans on racks for 2 minutes. Transfer to racks; let cool.

128

Makes about 80 pieces. PER PIECE: about 42 cal, 1 g pro, 3 g total fat (1 g sat. fat), 4 g carb, trace fibre, 12 mg chol, 57 mg sodium. % RDI: 1% iron, 3% vit A, 3% folate.

Olive Pesto Biscotti

Black olive–studded biscotti make great partners for martinis or red wine.

½ cup **pesto**

¼ cup **butter,** softened

2 **eggs**

¼ cup **milk**

3 cups **all-purpose flour**

2 tsp **baking powder**

¼ tsp **salt**

¾ cup quartered **black olives**

1 **egg white**

In large bowl, beat pesto with butter until fluffy; beat in eggs and milk. Whisk together flour, baking powder and salt; stir into butter mixture. Stir in olives. Whisk egg white with 1 tbsp water.

On lightly floured surface, form dough into four 7-inch (18 cm) long logs. Place, 3 inches (8 cm) apart, on 2 parchment paper–lined or greased rimless baking sheets. Brush tops with egg white mixture.

Bake in top and bottom thirds of 350°F (180°C) oven, rotating and switching pans halfway through, until light golden and firm, 30 minutes. Let cool on pans on racks for 10 minutes.

Transfer logs to cutting board. Using serrated knife, cut diagonally into ½-inch (1 cm) thick slices; stand upright, ½ inch (1 cm) apart, on prepared pans. Bake in top and bottom thirds of oven, rotating and switching pans halfway through, until cut sides are light golden and dry, 40 minutes. Let cool on pans on racks for 2 minutes. Transfer to racks; let cool. *(Make-ahead: Layer between waxed paper in airtight container and store for up to 5 days or freeze for up to 3 weeks.)*

129

Makes about 46 pieces. PER PIECE: about 55 cal, 1 g pro, 2 g total fat (1 g sat. fat), 7 g carb, trace fibre, 11 mg chol, 86 mg sodium. % RDI: 1% calcium, 4% iron, 2% vit A, 8% folate.

PESTO BAGEL CRISPS

Coin-size slices of bagels make easy, bite-size bases for toppings.

Place 2 unsliced plain or pumpernickel bagels on cutting board. Cut each bagel vertically into about 24 thin coin-size rounds. Spread rounds in single layer on large rimmed baking sheet.

Stir 2 tbsp vegetable oil with 4 tsp pesto; brush over both sides of rounds. Toast in 350°F (180°C) oven until golden and crisp, about 12 minutes. Let cool on pan on rack. *(Make-ahead: Store in airtight container for up to 3 days.)*

Makes 48 pieces. PER PIECE: about 16 cal, trace pro, 1 g total fat (0 g sat. fat), 2 g carb, 0 g fibre, 0 mg chol, 23 mg sodium. % RDI: 1% iron, 1% folate.

130

PITA CRUNCHIES

Serve these addictive chips in a bowl along with your favourite sour cream–based dip.

Using scissors, trim 4 pitas (each 6 inches/15 cm) around edges to make 2 rounds each. Brush 3 tbsp extra-virgin olive oil over rough sides. Halve 1 clove garlic; rub cut sides over rounds.

Cut each into 6 triangles; arrange, oiled side up, in single layer on rimmed baking sheets. Sprinkle with ¾ tsp cumin seeds and ½ tsp coarse sea salt, pressing to adhere.

Bake in 350°F (180°C) oven until crisp and golden, about 12 minutes. *(Make-ahead: Store in airtight container for up to 1 week.)*

Makes 48 pieces. PER PIECE: about 21 cal, trace pro, 1 g total fat (trace sat. fat), 3 g carb, trace fibre, 0 mg chol, 43 mg sodium. % RDI: 1% iron, 1% folate.

CROÛTES

Squares, triangles, rounds or stars – cut whatever shape you like.

Using rolling pin, flatten 18 slices bread (white, raisin, whole wheat or rye). Using 2-inch (5 cm) fluted or plain round cutter, cut 2 rounds from each slice; reserve trimmings for another use, such as bread crumbs. Lightly brush both sides of rounds with 3 tbsp butter, melted.

Toast on rimmed baking sheet in 350°F (180°C) oven until golden and crisp, 12 to 14 minutes. Let cool on pan on rack. *(Make-ahead: Store in airtight container for up to 3 days. To recrisp, if necessary, bake in 350°F/180°C oven for about 5 minutes.)*

Makes 36 pieces. PER PIECE: about 32 cal, 1 g pro, 1 g total fat (1 g sat. fat), 4 g carb, trace fibre, 3 mg chol, 57 mg sodium. % RDI: 1% calcium, 2% iron, 1% vit A, 3% folate.

TOAST CUPS

Croûtes made into cups are great containers for all sorts of savoury fillings.

Trim crusts off 18 slices bread (white, raisin, whole wheat or rye); using rolling pin, roll each slice until about ⅛ inch (3 mm) thick. Using 2-inch (5 cm) round cookie cutter, cut 2 rounds from each slice; reserve trimmings for another use, such as bread crumbs.

Brush rounds with 1 tbsp vegetable oil; press into 1½-inch (4 cm) tart tins to form shells. Bake in 350°F (180°C) oven until crisp and golden, 10 to 15 minutes. Let cool on pans on racks. *(Make-ahead: Store in airtight container for up to 1 week or freeze for up to 1 month.)*

Makes 36 pieces. PER PIECE: about 14 cal, trace pro, 1 g total fat (0 g sat. fat), 2 g carb, trace fibre, 0 mg chol, 22 mg sodium, 5 mg potassium. % RDI: 1% iron, 2% folate.

CROSTINI

Day-old baguette (white or whole grain) works best for these because it's easier to slice than fresh.

Cut baguette into forty ⅓-inch (8 mm) thick slices. Broil on rimmed baking sheet, turning once, until golden and crisp, about 1½ minutes. *(Make-ahead: Let cool. Store in airtight container for up to 3 days.)*

Makes 40 pieces. PER PIECE: about 13 cal, trace pro, trace total fat (0 g sat. fat), 2 g carb, trace fibre, 0 mg chol, 28 mg sodium. % RDI: 1% iron, 1% folate.

Change It Up

BRUSCHETTA

Halve large clove garlic. Toast baguette slices as directed; let cool. Lightly rub 1 side of each slice with cut sides of garlic; brush with extra-virgin olive oil, if desired. *(Make-ahead: Store in airtight container for up to 3 days.)*

PITA CRISPS

Thin pita wedges make tasty scoops for dips.

In small bowl, combine ¼ cup vegetable oil and ¼ tsp each salt and paprika; set aside.

Using scissors, trim 3 pitas (each 6 inches/15 cm) around edges to make 2 rounds each; brush oil mixture over rough sides of rounds.

Cut each round into 8 wedges; arrange, oiled side up, in single layer on large rimmed baking sheet.

Bake in 350°F (180°C) oven until golden and crisp, about 12 minutes. Let cool on pan on rack. *(Make-ahead: Store in airtight container for up to 3 days.)*

Makes 48 pieces. PER PIECE: about 20 cal, trace pro, 1 g total fat (0 g sat. fat), 2 g carb, 0 g fibre, 0 mg chol, 32 mg sodium. % RDI: 1% iron, 1% folate.

131

Poppy Seed Crackers

Delicious on their own, these tuile-like crisps also make perfect platforms for all sorts of dips and spreads.

⅓ cup **butter,** softened

½ cup **all-purpose flour**

3 **egg whites**

2 tbsp **grainy mustard**

1 tbsp **poppy seeds**

¼ tsp each **salt** and **pepper**

In large bowl, beat butter with flour until smooth. Add egg whites, mustard, poppy seeds, salt and pepper; beat until thickened, about 3 minutes.

Drop by six 1 tbsp mounds, about 5 inches (12 cm) apart, onto parchment paper–lined rimless baking sheets. Using small offset spatula or knife, spread each into 3-inch (8 cm) circle.

Bake, 1 sheet at a time, in 325°F (160°C) oven until golden around edges, about 18 minutes. Let cool on pan on rack for 2 minutes. Transfer to rack; let cool. *(Make-ahead: Store in airtight container for up to 1 week.)*

132

Makes about 20 pieces. PER PIECE: about 45 cal, 1 g pro, 3 g total fat (2 g sat. fat), 3 g carb, trace fibre, 10 mg chol, 88 mg sodium. % RDI: 1% calcium, 1% iron, 3% vit A, 3% folate.

Lavash

Rolling out the dough until it's paper-thin makes for the crispiest lavash.

1½ cups **bread flour**

½ tsp **salt**

½ tsp **quick-rising (instant) dry yeast**

2 tbsp **vegetable oil**

2 tsp **liquid honey**

½ cup **warm water**

1 tsp **caraway seeds**

1 tsp **poppy seeds**

½ tsp **kosher salt** or coarse sea salt

In bowl, whisk together flour, salt and yeast; stir in oil and honey. Stir in warm water to form stiff dough.

Turn out onto lightly floured surface; knead until smooth, about 5 minutes. Place in greased bowl, turning to grease all over; cover and let rise in warm, draft-free place until doubled in bulk, about 1½ hours.

Turn out onto lightly floured surface; roll out into 17- x 12-inch (42 x 30 cm) paper-thin rectangle. Transfer to large greased or parchment paper–lined rimless baking sheet; gently stretch edges to hang ½ inch (1 cm) over sides of pan. Let rest for 5 minutes; release edges, letting overhang shrink back.

Lightly brush top with water; sprinkle with caraway seeds, poppy seeds and salt. Bake in 375°F (190°C) oven until golden and crisp, 16 to 20 minutes. Let cool on pan on rack. Break into long shards. *(Make-ahead: Store in airtight container for up to 1 week.)*

133

Makes 1 sheet, or 16 pieces. PER PIECE: about 66 cal, 2 g pro, 2 g total fat (trace sat. fat), 10 g carb, trace fibre, 0 mg chol, 121 mg sodium. % RDI: 1% calcium, 4% iron, 8% folate.

CHAPTER 5

TINY
sandwiches

From left: Shrimp Sliders With Wasabi-Lime Mayo (page 158) and Mini-Cheeseburgers (page 159)

Grilled Panzanella Bites

This appetizer is a fun way to serve a popular Italian bread salad. Tomatoes are supersweet when in season, and taste best when kept at room temperature, so buy or pick them right before you need them.

⅓ cup **olive oil**

¼ cup **red wine vinegar** or white wine vinegar

2 cloves **garlic,** minced

½ tsp **salt**

¼ tsp **pepper**

1 cup **mini pearl bocconcini**

½ cup finely chopped **red onion**

1 **baguette** (24 inches/60 cm), diagonally cut in ½-inch (1 cm) thick slices

4 cups halved **grape tomatoes**

½ cup chopped **fresh basil**

In bowl, whisk together ¼ cup of the oil, vinegar, garlic, salt and pepper. Add bocconcini and onion; cover and refrigerate for 2 hours. *(Make-ahead: Refrigerate for up to 24 hours.)*

Brush remaining oil over both sides of baguette slices. Place on greased grill over medium heat; grill, turning occasionally, until crisp and golden, about 5 minutes.

Meanwhile, add tomatoes and basil to cheese mixture; toss to combine. Serve on toasted baguette slices.

Change It Up

GRILLED VILLAGE SALAD BITES

Omit salt. Replace bocconcini with ¾ cup crumbled feta cheese. Replace basil with mint. Add ⅓ cup chopped Kalamata olives along with tomatoes.

Makes 24 pieces. PER PIECE: about 94 cal, 3 g pro, 5 g total fat (2 g sat. fat), 9 g carb, 1 g fibre, 6 mg chol, 138 mg sodium, 75 mg potassium. % RDI: 5% calcium, 4% iron, 3% vit A, 5% vit C, 7% folate.

Curried Chicken Melts

Firm, thin sandwich bread is ideal for these party pleasers. They look prettiest when the bread is cut before topping; if you're in a hurry, though, you can top the whole slices, then bake and cut into triangles.

2 cups diced **cooked chicken**

3 tbsp **light mayonnaise**

1 rib **celery,** finely diced

2 **green onions,** finely diced

2 tsp **lemon juice**

1 tsp **curry powder**

¼ tsp each **salt** and **pepper**

7 slices **firm white sandwich bread**
or whole wheat sandwich bread

¾ cup shredded **Cheddar cheese**

Stir together chicken, mayonnaise, celery, green onions, lemon juice, curry powder, salt and pepper.

On baking sheet, broil bread for 1 minute. Turn over; cut each slice into 4 triangles.

Divide chicken mixture among triangles; sprinkle with cheese. Broil until cheese is melted and bubbly, about 3 minutes.

138

Makes 28 pieces. PER PIECE: about 59 cal, 4 g pro, 3 g total fat (1 g sat. fat), 5 g carb, trace fibre, 13 mg chol, 105 mg sodium, 46 mg potassium. % RDI: 3% calcium, 3% iron, 1% vit A, 5% folate.

Pomegranate Brie Bites

The pomegranate syrup topping these canapés is simple to make, and any extras are wonderful drizzled over desserts, cheeses and grilled meats. If it becomes too thick, just loosen with a few drops of warm water.

1 cup **100% pomegranate juice**

2 tbsp **granulated sugar**

¼ cup **olive oil**

1 **baguette** (24 inches/60 cm), cut diagonally in ½-inch (1 cm) thick slices

7 oz (200 g) double- or triple-cream **Brie cheese**

3 **fresh figs** (such as Black Mission)

24 **pecan halves,** toasted

In small saucepan, bring pomegranate juice and sugar to boil over high heat; boil until syrupy and reduced to ¼ cup, about 20 minutes.

Meanwhile, brush oil over both sides of baguette slices. Arrange on baking sheet; broil, turning once, until golden, 2 to 4 minutes.

Cut Brie cheese into 24 slices; divide evenly among toasts. Cut each fig into 8 wedges; place 1 wedge on each cheese slice. Top each with pecan. *(Make-ahead: Refrigerate in airtight container for up to 24 hours.)*

Broil until cheese is bubbly, about 1 minute. Transfer to serving platter; drizzle each piece with ½ tsp of the pomegranate syrup.

139

Makes **24 pieces.** PER PIECE: about 117 cal, 3 g pro, 8 g total fat (2 g sat. fat), 12 g carb, 1 g fibre, 10 mg chol, 140 mg sodium, 64 mg potassium. % RDI: 6% calcium, 4% iron, 2% vit A, 6% folate.

Smashed Pea Crostini

The classic combination of mint and peas makes for a lovely summery appetizer bursting with fresh flavours.

1 **baguette** (24 inches/60 cm), cut in ½-inch (1 cm) thick slices

⅓ cup **extra-virgin olive oil**

1 cup shelled **fresh peas**

1 cup **ricotta cheese**

¼ cup grated **Parmesan cheese**

3 tbsp packed **fresh mint leaves**

2 tsp **lemon juice**

1 clove **garlic,** minced (optional)

½ tsp each **salt** and **pepper**

2 oz (55 g) **Parmesan cheese,** shaved

Arrange baguette slices on baking sheet. Brush 2 tbsp of the oil over both sides. Broil, turning once, until golden and crisp, about 2 minutes. Set aside.

In saucepan of boiling salted water, cook peas just until tender, 2 to 3 minutes. Drain and chill in ice water; drain well.

In food processor, purée together ricotta, remaining oil, grated Parmesan, mint, lemon juice, garlic (if using), salt and pepper. Pulse in peas until crushed but still chunky.

Top each crostini with some of the pea mixture; garnish with shaved Parmesan cheese.

141

How-To

SHAVING HARD CHEESES

Parmesan and other hard cheeses look (and taste) especially nice on salads and appetizers when they're shaved into curls. The simplest way to do this is to use the humble vegetable peeler. Just slide it down the narrow edge of the cheese to make pretty shavings.

Makes about 40 pieces. PER PIECE: about 56 cal, 2 g pro, 3 g total fat (1 g sat. fat), 4 g carb, 1 g fibre, 5 mg chol, 114 mg sodium, 28 mg potassium. % RDI: 4% calcium, 2% iron, 2% vit A, 2% vit C, 4% folate.

Tapenade Crostini

This zesty olive hors d'oeuvre is delicious on its own, but it's more decadent when the crostini is spread with a bit of goat cheese before it's topped with the tapenade.

¼ cup **extra-virgin olive oil**

1 **baguette** (24 inches/60 cm), cut diagonally in ½-inch (1 cm) thick slices

2 cups pitted **Kalamata olives,** rinsed

1 tsp **anchovy paste**

1 small **shallot,** chopped

1 clove **garlic,** minced

1 tsp rinsed drained **capers,** minced

½ tsp **pepper**

2 tbsp chopped **fresh parsley**

Brush half of the oil over both sides of baguette slices. Broil on baking sheet, turning once, until golden, 2 to 3 minutes. *(Make-ahead: Store in airtight container for up to 24 hours.)*

In food processor or by hand, coarsely chop together olives, remaining oil, anchovy paste, shallot, garlic, capers and pepper. Stir in parsley. *(Make-ahead: Refrigerate in airtight container for up to 3 days.)*

Top each crostini with scant 1 tbsp of the tapenade.

142

Makes **24 pieces.** PER PIECE: about 88 cal, 1 g pro, 7 g total fat (1 g sat. fat), 7 g carb, 1 g fibre, 0 mg chol, 446 mg sodium, 21 mg potassium. % RDI: 2% calcium, 4% iron, 4% folate.

Reuben Canapés

The old-school deli sandwich gets a new lease on life as an attractive appetizer. For a big party, make a platter of these and the tasty variations.

Half **baguette** (12 inches/30 cm for half)

2 tbsp **extra-virgin olive oil**

¼ tsp each **salt** and **pepper**

TOPPING:

2 tbsp **Dijon mustard**

⅔ cup drained **jarred sauerkraut**

12 thin slices **Montreal smoked meat** or corned beef (8 oz/225 g), cut in half

24 small slices **Gruyère cheese**

Cut baguette into twenty-four ¼-inch (5 mm) thick slices; place on baking sheet. Brush oil over tops of baguette slices; sprinkle with salt and pepper. Broil, turning once, until crisp and golden, about 3 minutes.

TOPPING: Brush oiled sides of toasts with mustard. Top each with about 1 tsp of the sauerkraut, half-slice of the meat and 1 slice of the cheese. If desired, broil until cheese is bubbly and melted, 1 minute.

143

Change It Up

GOAT CHEESE & ROASTED RED PEPPER CANAPÉS

Omit Topping. Top each toast with about 1 tsp soft goat cheese, 1 small strip drained jarred roasted red pepper and half black olive.

PESTO SALAMI CANAPÉS

Omit Topping. Top each toast with about ½ tsp pesto, half-slice salami, 1 fresh basil leaf and 1 slice bocconcini cheese.

SMOKED TROUT & BOURSIN CANAPÉS

Omit Topping. Top each toast with 1 tsp Herb and Garlic Boursin cheese, 1 slice English cucumber and 1 small piece hot-smoked trout or salmon. Sprinkle toasts with 2 tbsp chopped fresh chives.

LIVER PÂTÉ & CARAMELIZED ONION CANAPÉS

Omit Topping. In large skillet, heat 2 tbsp vegetable oil over medium-low heat. Cook 1 Spanish onion, thinly sliced; ½ tsp dried thyme; and pinch each salt and pepper until onions are golden, about 30 minutes. Top each toast with about 1 tsp liver pâté, scant ¼ tsp red currant jelly and about 1 tsp of the caramelized onion mixture.

Makes 24 pieces. PER PIECE: about 53 cal, 3 g pro, 3 g total fat (1 g sat. fat), 3 g carb, trace fibre, 12 mg chol, 241 mg sodium. % RDI: 3% calcium, 4% iron, 1% vit A, 2% vit C, 3% folate.

Atlantic Shrimp Salad on Rye

Sustainable Atlantic (cold-water) shrimp are so tender and sweet. This simple herbed salad makes a wonderful plated appetizer for eight, but it's just as fantastic turned into canapés on cocktail rye bread.

2 pkg (12 oz/340 g each)
  frozen cooked peeled cold-water shrimp, thawed

¼ cup **light mayonnaise**

2 tbsp **lemon juice**

1 tbsp each chopped **fresh parsley, fresh chives** and **fresh dill**

1 **green onion,** thinly sliced

¼ tsp **pepper**

Pinch **salt**

8 leaves **Boston lettuce**

1 cup thinly sliced **radishes**

8 slices **rye bread** or sourdough bread

1 oz (30 g) **pea sprouts**

Place shrimp between 2 paper towels and pat dry, gently pressing out any liquid.

In bowl, stir together shrimp, mayonnaise, lemon juice, parsley, chives, dill, green onion, pepper and salt.

Divide lettuce, shrimp mixture and radishes among slices of bread. Garnish with pea sprouts.

145

Change It Up

ATLANTIC SHRIMP SALAD ON COCKTAIL RYE

Substitute cocktail rye bread (squares or rounds) for rye bread; tear lettuce into pieces. Top each cocktail rye with 1 piece of the lettuce, then rounded 1 tbsp of the shrimp salad. **Makes about 30 pieces.**

Makes 8 servings. PER SERVING: about 198 cal, 21 g pro, 5 g total fat (1 g sat. fat), 17 g carb, 3 g fibre, 132 mg chol, 381 mg sodium, 277 mg potassium. % RDI: 7% calcium, 23% iron, 9% vit A, 16% vit C, 22% folate.

Brie Canapés With Cranberry Pear Chutney

This recipe makes about 1½ cups chutney, enough for 72 pieces. Refrigerate any leftover chutney for up to 2 weeks to use on canapés or cheese plates, or as an accompaniment to curries and meat pies.

24 slices **baguette,** toasted, or other crackers or toasts

8 oz (225 g) **Brie cheese** or Camembert cheese, cut in 24 slices

CRANBERRY PEAR CHUTNEY:

2 tsp **black mustard seeds** or yellow mustard seeds

¼ tsp **cumin seeds**

1 cup fresh or frozen **cranberries,** halved or coarsely chopped

½ cup finely diced **dried pears**

½ cup finely diced **sweet onion**

¼ cup packed **brown sugar**

3 tbsp **cider vinegar**

2 tsp minced **fresh ginger**

¼ tsp **ground cloves**

Pinch each **cayenne pepper** and **salt**

CRANBERRY PEAR CHUTNEY: In small saucepan, toast mustard and cumin seeds over medium-low heat until mustard seeds just begin to pop, about 5 minutes. Add cranberries, pears, onion, brown sugar, vinegar, ginger, cloves, cayenne pepper, salt and ¼ cup water. Bring to simmer; reduce heat and simmer, covered and stirring occasionally, until mixture is thick and jamlike, about 40 minutes. Let cool.

Top each baguette toast with 1 cheese slice; top each with 1 tsp chutney.

146

Makes 24 pieces. PER PIECE: about 55 cal, 3 g pro, 3 g total fat (2 g sat. fat), 4 g carb, trace fibre, 10 mg chol, 90 mg sodium, 37 mg potassium. % RDI: 2% calcium, 1% iron, 2% vit A, 5% folate.

Apple Pork Tenderloin Canapés

Choose a long, thin baguette with a crisp crust for these hors d'oeuvres. Granny Smith apples are tangy and go well with the pork.

3 tbsp **apple jelly**

1 tbsp **vegetable oil**

1 tbsp **balsamic vinegar**

½ tsp **dried thyme**

½ tsp each **salt** and **pepper**

1 **pork tenderloin** (12 oz/340 g)

Half **green-skinned apple**

2 tbsp **lemon juice**

⅓ cup **light cream cheese,** softened

24 thin slices **baguette,** toasted

In bowl, combine 1 tbsp of the apple jelly, the oil, vinegar, half of the thyme, the salt and pepper; add pork, turning to coat. Cover and refrigerate for 30 minutes. *(Make-ahead: Refrigerate for up to 24 hours.)*

Place pork in small roasting pan, tucking small end under. Roast in 425°F (220°C) oven until just a hint of pink remains inside, about 20 minutes. Tent with foil; let stand for 10 minutes before slicing thinly. *(Make-ahead: Let cool. Refrigerate in airtight container for up to 2 days.)*

Core and thinly slice apple; cut each slice in half. Toss apple slices with lemon juice to prevent browning. Whisk together cream cheese, and remaining apple jelly and thyme until smooth.

Spread 1 tsp cheese mixture over each toast. Overlap 2 apple slices on top; curl pork slice decoratively over apple.

147

Makes 24 pieces. PER PIECE: about 47 cal, 3 g pro, 1 g total fat (1 g sat. fat), 5 g carb, trace fibre, 8 mg chol, 102 mg sodium. % RDI: 1% calcium, 2% iron, 2% vit C, 2% folate.

Smashed Beans on Toast

Rustic and garlicky, this is a simple yet fantastic Mediterranean-inspired open-faced sandwich. Serve with extra olive oil to drizzle over top.

⅓ cup **extra-virgin olive oil**

1 **sourdough baguette**
(24 inches/60 cm), cut
diagonally in 32 slices

3 cloves **garlic,** minced

3 cups **cooked white kidney
beans** (See How-To, below)

2 tsp minced **fresh sage** or parsley

½ tsp **salt**

½ cup **bean cooking liquid** or water

⅓ cup shaved **Parmesan cheese**

Brush 2 tbsp of the oil over top of baguette slices. Broil on rimmed baking sheet, turning once, until crisp and golden, about 2 minutes.

In skillet, heat remaining oil over medium heat; cook garlic, stirring, until fragrant, 30 seconds.

Stir in beans, sage and salt; cook, stirring, for 3 minutes, mashing with wooden spoon just until broken (not pasty). Stir in bean cooking liquid; cook, stirring, for 2 minutes. Spoon heaping 1 tbsp onto each toast; top with cheese.

149

How-To

COOKING DRIED BEANS

• You need to soak most dried legumes (or beans) before cooking. Rinse and soak them overnight in three times their volume of water. (To quick-soak them, bring beans and water to boil; boil gently for 2 minutes. Remove from heat, cover and let stand for 1 hour. Drain. Reduce cooking time by 5 to 10 minutes.)

• In saucepan, cover beans again with three times their volume of water; bring to boil. Reduce heat, cover and simmer until tender, 30 to 80 minutes, depending on bean variety (see Cooking Times, right). Drain, reserving cooking liquid to use in recipes.

• One cup dried beans simmers into about 2 cups cooked beans (up to ½ cup more depending on bean variety).

• Start checking beans by tasting them about 10 minutes before suggested cooking time and every 5 minutes thereafter. A well-cooked bean is tender and easy to squash in your mouth.

Cooking Times
• **Black beans:** 30 minutes
• **Black-eyed peas:** 35 minutes
• **Chickpeas:** 45 minutes
• **Kidney beans (white and red):** 50 minutes
• **Large lima beans:** 55 minutes
• **Navy beans:** 40 minutes
• **Romano beans:** 45 minutes

Makes 32 pieces. PER PIECE: about 70 cal, 3 g pro, 3 g total fat (1 g sat. fat), 8 g carb, 1 g fibre, 1 mg chol, 105 mg sodium. % RDI: 2% calcium, 4% iron, 13% folate.

Garlic Pâté on Toasts

Here's a simple canapé chock-full of mellow roasted garlic flavour. Add a pinch of chopped fresh chives, parsley, oregano or basil for colour.

3 heads **garlic**

1 cup cubed **white bread** (crusts removed)

2 tbsp **lemon juice**

¼ tsp **salt**

¼ cup **extra-virgin olive oil**

14 **black olives**, pitted and halved

Half drained **jarred roasted red pepper**, diced

TOASTS:

1 **baguette** (24 inches/60 cm), cut in ¼-inch (5 mm) thick slices

⅓ cup **extra-virgin olive oil**

½ tsp **pepper**

¼ tsp **salt**

TOASTS: Place baguette slices on rimmed baking sheet. Brush tops lightly with oil; sprinkle with pepper and salt. Bake in 450°F (230°C) oven until golden and crisp, 7 minutes. *(Make-ahead: Let cool. Store in airtight container for up to 2 days.)*

Wrap garlic in foil; bake in 450°F (230°C) oven until softened, about 30 minutes. Let cool.

Separate garlic cloves; cut off tops and squeeze pulp into food processor. Add cubed bread, lemon juice and salt; purée. With motor running, drizzle in oil in steady stream until smooth. *(Make-ahead: Refrigerate in airtight container for up to 24 hours.)*

Spread ½ tsp of the pâté on each toast; top half with olive halves and half with red pepper pieces.

150

Makes about 55 pieces. PER PIECE: about 42 cal, 1 g pro, 3 g total fat (trace sat. fat), 4 g carb, trace fibre, 0 mg chol, 65 mg sodium. % RDI: 1% calcium, 2% iron, 3% vit C, 2% folate.

Peameal Bacon Sliders

The classic Canadian peameal sandwich – now in bite-size form! Sliders are trendy, so the buns are easy to find; for a tasty change of pace, cut a loaf of focaccia in half horizontally, then cut into 1½-inch (4 cm) squares.

1 small **sweet onion** or Vidalia onion

2 tbsp **butter**

½ tsp each **salt** and **pepper**

½ cup **sodium-reduced chicken broth**

¼ cup **maple syrup**

¼ cup **grainy mustard**

2 tbsp **olive oil**

2 lb (900 g) **peameal bacon,** sliced ¼ inch (5 mm) thick

24 **mini hamburger (slider) buns** or small dinner rolls

24 **gherkins,** cornichons, small pickled peppers or cocktail onions

Cut onion into ¼-inch (5 mm) thick rings. In skillet, melt butter over medium heat; cook onion and half each of the salt and pepper until onion is softened, about 8 minutes.

Add broth; cook, stirring, until no liquid remains, about 8 minutes. Set aside and keep warm.

Stir together maple syrup, mustard and remaining salt and pepper; set aside.

In nonstick skillet, heat half of the oil over medium-high heat; cook peameal bacon, in batches and adding remaining oil as necessary, turning once, until tender and golden, about 4 minutes. Cut each slice into 4 pieces. Add to maple mixture; toss to coat. (*Make-ahead: Refrigerate onion and bacon mixtures in separate airtight containers for up to 24 hours. Reheat onions.*)

Cut buns in half horizontally, if necessary; broil, cut side up, on baking sheet until golden and toasted, about 1 minute.

In saucepan, warm bacon mixture over medium heat, 1 to 3 minutes. Stack 4 pieces bacon on each bottom bun; top with onions, then top bun. Secure with gherkin-skewered toothpick.

151

Makes 24 pieces. PER PIECE: about 207 cal, 11 g pro, 7 g total fat (2 g sat. fat), 26 g carb, 1 g fibre, 21 mg chol, 981 mg sodium, 194 mg potassium. % RDI: 4% calcium, 10% iron, 1% vit A, 2% vit C, 12% folate.

Chicken Avocado Sandwiches With Lime Mayo

Dress up these sammies for a party with frilly picks and a little pickle or olive.

¼ cup **lime juice**

¼ cup **olive oil**

½ tsp each **salt, pepper** and **hot pepper flakes**

4 **boneless skinless chicken breasts** (about 6 oz/ 170 g each)

16 slices **white sandwich bread** or whole wheat sandwich bread

2 **ripe avocados**

LIME MAYO:

⅔ cup **light mayonnaise**

½ tsp grated **lime zest**

2 tbsp **lime juice**

¼ tsp each **hot pepper flakes, ground cumin** and **salt**

In shallow dish, stir together lime juice, oil, salt, pepper and hot pepper flakes; add chicken, turning to coat. Cover and refrigerate for 2 hours.

Place chicken on greased grill over medium-high heat; close lid and grill, turning once, until no longer pink inside, 15 to 20 minutes. Let cool. *(Make ahead: Cover and refrigerate for up to 8 hours.)* Cut crosswise into ¼-inch (5 mm) thick slices. Set aside.

LIME MAYO: Stir together mayonnaise, lime zest, lime juice, hot pepper flakes, cumin and salt; spread on bread slices.

Peel, pit and thinly slice avocados; sandwich avocado and chicken slices in bread, pressing lightly. Trim off crusts. Cut each sandwich into 4 squares or triangles; secure each with toothpick.

How-To

STORING TEA SANDWICHES OVERNIGHT

If you like, you can make tea sandwiches a day ahead. Just use this old catering trick to keep them fresh: Place the trimmed, cut sandwiches on a baking sheet; cover with a tea towel or paper towels that have just barely been spritzed with water. Cover tightly with plastic wrap and refrigerate for up to 24 hours.

152

Makes 32 pieces. PER PIECE: about 100 cal, 6 g pro, 5 g total fat (1 g sat. fat), 9 g carb, 1 g fibre, 14 mg chol, 146 mg sodium, 141 mg potassium. % RDI: 2% calcium, 4% iron, 1% vit A, 3% vit C, 11% folate.

From left: Chicken Avocado
Sandwiches With Lime Mayo
(opposite) and Egg Salad Finger
Sandwiches (page 154)

Egg Salad Finger Sandwiches

Cumin and green onion update this tea party favourite. Most of the ingredients are pantry staples, so these are perfect last-minute treats.

8 **hard-cooked eggs** (see How-To, below), peeled

⅓ cup **light mayonnaise**

1 **green onion,** thinly sliced

1 tsp **Dijon mustard**

½ tsp **ground cumin**

¼ tsp **pepper**

Pinch **salt**

⅓ cup **butter,** softened

16 thin slices **whole wheat sandwich bread** or white sandwich bread

Finely chop or coarsely grate eggs. Mix together eggs, mayonnaise, green onion, mustard, cumin, pepper and salt.

Spread butter on bread slices; sandwich egg mixture in bread, pressing lightly. Trim off crusts. Cut each sandwich into 4 rectangles. *(Make-ahead: To store overnight, see How-To, page 152.)*

154

How-To

HARD-COOKING EGGS

Arrange eggs in single layer in saucepan; pour in enough cold water to come 1 inch (2.5 cm) above eggs. Cover and bring to boil over high heat. Immediately remove from heat; let stand for 15 minutes. Drain and chill eggs under cold water for 2 minutes.

Makes 32 pieces. PER PIECE: about 79 cal, 3 g pro, 5 g total fat (2 g sat. fat), 7 g carb, 1 g fibre, 60 mg chol, 122 mg sodium, 55 mg potassium. % RDI: 2% calcium, 5% iron, 4% vit A, 6% folate.

Confetti Tea Sandwiches

Pimiento cheese is a much-loved sandwich filling in the southern United States. This version uses pimiento-stuffed olives for extra savouriness.

1 pkg (250 g) **cream cheese,** softened

⅓ cup **light mayonnaise**

1 cup shredded **extra-old Cheddar cheese**

⅓ cup **pimiento-stuffed green olives,** chopped

2 tbsp chopped **fresh parsley**

¼ tsp **pepper**

⅓ cup **butter,** softened

16 thin slices **white sandwich bread** or whole wheat sandwich bread

In bowl, beat cream cheese with mayonnaise until smooth; stir in Cheddar cheese, olives, parsley and pepper.

Spread butter over bread slices; sandwich cheese mixture in bread, pressing lightly. Trim off crusts. Cut each sandwich into 4 squares or triangles. *(Make-ahead: To store overnight, see How-To, page 152.)*

155

Makes 32 pieces. PER PIECE: about 106 cal, 3 g pro, 7 g total fat (4 g sat. fat), 8 g carb, trace fibre, 18 mg chol, 172 mg sodium, 33 mg potassium. % RDI: 4% calcium, 4% iron, 6% vit A, 7% folate.

Shrimp & Avocado Salad Cucumber Bites

Fresh cold-water shrimp salad on a slice of crisp, cool cucumber makes a refreshing summer hors d'oeuvre with a glass of chilled rosé.

1 **firm ripe avocado**

Half pkg (12 oz/340 g pkg) **frozen cooked peeled cold-water shrimp,** thawed and chopped

2 tbsp chopped **fresh parsley**

2 tbsp **light mayonnaise**

1 tbsp **lemon juice**

½ tsp **salt**

¼ tsp **pepper**

1 **English cucumber,** cut diagonally in 24 slices

Pit, peel and dice avocado. Stir together avocado, shrimp, parsley, mayonnaise, lemon juice, salt and pepper.

Spoon about 1 tbsp of the shrimp salad onto each cucumber slice.

157

Makes 24 pieces. PER PIECE: about 27 cal, 2 g pro, 2 g total fat (trace sat. fat), 2 g carb, 1 g fibre, 14 mg chol, 73 mg sodium, 79 mg potassium. % RDI: 1% calcium, 2% iron, 1% vit A, 3% vit C, 4% folate.

Shrimp Sliders With Wasabi Lime Mayo

These sliders sound fussy, but they come together so quickly thanks to a food processor. Cover and keep the finished patties warm while the other batches cook.

½ cup **fresh bread crumbs**

1 **egg**

2 cloves **garlic**

2 **green onions**

Pinch each **salt** and **pepper**

1 lb (450 g) **frozen peeled raw shrimp,** thawed

1 tbsp **vegetable oil**

¼ cup chopped **fresh cilantro**

12 **mini hamburger (slider) buns**

WASABI LIME MAYO:

⅓ cup **mayonnaise**

½ tsp grated **lime zest**

2 tbsp **lime juice**

1 tsp **wasabi paste**

¼ tsp **pepper**

In food processor, pulse together bread crumbs, egg, garlic, green onions, salt and pepper until onions are finely chopped. Add shrimp; continue to pulse until finely chopped. Scoop by scant ¼ cup, pressing lightly to make ¾-inch (2 cm) thick patties. *(Make-ahead: Layer between waxed paper in airtight container and refrigerate for up to 12 hours.)*

In large nonstick skillet, heat oil over medium-high heat; cook patties, in batches and turning once, until golden and firm, about 4 minutes.

WASABI LIME MAYO: Meanwhile, stir together mayonnaise, lime zest, lime juice, wasabi and pepper. *(Make-ahead: Cover and refrigerate for up to 2 days.)*

Sandwich patties, mayo and cilantro in buns.

How-To

SHAPING PERFECT PATTIES

Eyeballing the amount of shrimp mixture per patty can result in a variety of sizes. If you use a measuring cup for each one, you'll end up with nice, uniform results. The mixture is quite sticky, so wet your hands before pressing the patties into shape to keep them smooth.

Makes 12 pieces. PER PIECE: about 176 cal, 10 g pro, 9 g total fat (2 g sat. fat), 14 g carb, 1 g fibre, 84 mg chol, 203 mg sodium, 94 mg potassium. % RDI: 3% calcium, 13% iron, 5% vit A, 3% vit C, 4% folate.

Mini-Cheeseburgers

Serve these little burgers with dill pickle spears. Dab any kind of mustard you like onto the burgers – Dijon, grainy, Russian, hot English or plain-old yellow are all delicious.

1 **egg**

¼ cup **dry bread crumbs**

1 small **onion,** grated

2 tbsp **sweet green relish**

1 tsp **Worcestershire sauce**

½ tsp each **dried oregano, salt** and **pepper**

1 lb (450 g) **lean ground beef**

2 oz (55 g) sliced **Swiss cheese,** Cheddar cheese or mozzarella cheese

32 **mini-pitas**

2 tbsp **mustard** (approx)

½ cup **cherry tomatoes,** sliced

1 tbsp minced **fresh parsley**

In bowl, whisk together egg, bread crumbs, ¼ cup water, onion, relish, Worcestershire sauce, oregano, salt and pepper; mix in beef. Form by rounded 1 tbsp into ¼-inch (5 mm) thick patties. (*Make-ahead: Layer between waxed paper in airtight container and refrigerate for up to 1 day. Or freeze for up to 4 weeks; thaw in refrigerator.*)

Place patties on foil-lined rimmed baking sheet; bake in 375°F (190°C) oven until no longer pink inside, about 10 minutes. Meanwhile, cut cheese into 1-inch (2.5 cm) squares; set aside.

Cut one-third off edge of each pita; open to form pocket. Stuff each with patty; top each with dab of mustard; top with 1 cheese square. Place on baking sheet. (*Make-ahead: Cover with plastic wrap; refrigerate for up to 24 hours.*)

Add cherry tomato slice and sprinkle of parsley to each pocket. Bake in 375°F (190°C) oven until cheese is melted, 5 to 10 minutes.

159

Makes 32 pieces. PER PIECE: about 57 cal, 4 g pro, 2 g total fat (1 g sat. fat), 5 g carb, trace fibre, 15 mg chol, 105 mg sodium. % RDI: 2% calcium, 4% iron, 1% vit A, 2% vit C, 3% folate.

Mini-Cubanos

A typical Miami-style cubano sandwich calls for a large pork roast. Marinated pork tenderloin speeds things up in this shortcut mini-version.

¼ cup **butter,** softened

12 thick (½ inch/1 cm) slices **French bread** or Italian bread

2 tbsp **mustard** (optional)

12 slices **Swiss cheese**

6 slices **Black Forest ham**

12 slices **dill pickle**

MARINATED PORK TENDERLOIN:

⅓ cup finely chopped **onion**

¼ cup **orange juice**

¼ cup **olive oil**

1 tbsp **lemon juice**

1 tbsp **lime juice**

1 clove **garlic,** minced

¼ tsp each **salt** and **dried oregano**

1 lb (450 g) **pork tenderloin**

MARINATED PORK TENDERLOIN: In shallow baking dish or resealable bag, stir together onion, orange juice, oil, lemon juice, lime juice, garlic, salt and oregano; add pork, turning to coat. Cover or seal and refrigerate for 4 hours. *(Make-ahead: Marinate for up to 24 hours.)*

Place pork on greased grill over medium-high heat. Close lid and grill, turning occasionally, until juices run clear when pork is pierced and just a hint of pink remains inside, 20 to 25 minutes. Let stand for 10 minutes. *(Make-ahead: Cover and refrigerate for up to 24 hours.)*

Cut pork into ¼-inch (5 mm) thick slices. Spread butter on 1 side of each bread slice. Spread mustard (if using) on other side. Turn half of the slices buttered side down; top each with 1 slice of the cheese, 1 slice of the ham, 2 slices of the pickle, a few slices of the pork and another slice of the cheese. Top with remaining bread, buttered side up.

Using panini press, or in greased skillet over medium heat, grill sandwiches until cheese is melted, about 10 minutes. Cut each sandwich into quarters.

Makes 24 pieces. PER PIECE: about 116 cal, 9 g pro, 6 g total fat (3 g sat. fat), 7 g carb, trace fibre, 27 mg chol, 203 mg sodium, 100 mg potassium. % RDI: 8% calcium, 4% iron, 4% vit A, 5% folate.

Open-Faced Cucumber Tea Sandwiches

Thin, crisp slices of cucumber top these dainty herbed-butter bites.

2 tbsp **butter,** softened

1 tbsp each finely chopped **fresh chives** and **fresh parsley**

Pinch **pepper**

6 thin slices **white sandwich bread** or whole wheat sandwich bread

36 thin slices small **English cucumber**

12 **fresh parsley leaves**

Stir together butter, chives, chopped parsley and pepper.

Using 2-inch (5 cm) round or fluted cookie cutter, cut 2 rounds from each bread slice. Spread each with butter mixture. *(Make-ahead: Cover with plastic wrap and refrigerate for up to 4 hours.)*

Arrange 3 cucumber slices in concentric circle over butter. Top each with parsley leaf.

163

Makes 12 pieces. PER PIECE: about 31 cal, 1 g pro, 2 g total fat (1 g sat. fat), 3 g carb, trace fibre, 5 mg chol, 40 mg sodium. % RDI: 1% calcium, 1% iron, 2% vit A, 2% vit C, 3% folate.

Tuna Melt Bites

A diner favourite becomes a cocktail party hero. Make a double batch – these teensy open-faced sandwiches will disappear quickly.

12 slices **rye bread**

1 tbsp **olive oil**

½ cup finely diced **onion**

¼ cup each finely diced **celery** and **sweet red pepper**

½ tsp **dried oregano**

2 cans (each 6 oz/170 g) **flaked white tuna,** drained

½ cup **light mayonnaise**

¼ tsp each **salt** and **pepper**

½ cup shredded **old Cheddar cheese**

2 tbsp thinly sliced **green onion** (green part only) or chives

With 2-inch (5 cm) round cutter, cut 24 circles from bread. Bake on foil-lined baking sheet in 350°F (180°C) oven, turning once, until golden, about 10 minutes. *(Make-ahead: Store in airtight container for up to 24 hours.)*

In skillet, heat oil over medium heat; cook onion, celery, red pepper and oregano, stirring occasionally, until softened, about 4 minutes.

In bowl, mash tuna; mix in mayonnaise, salt, pepper and vegetable mixture. *(Make-ahead: Cover and refrigerate for up to 24 hours.)*

Place rounded 1 tbsp tuna mixture on each toast; spread to edge. Sprinkle with cheese. Broil on foil-lined baking sheet until cheese is bubbly, about 1½ minutes. Sprinkle with green onion.

164

Makes 24 pieces. PER PIECE: about 58 cal, 4 g pro, 4 g total fat (1 g sat. fat), 3 g carb, trace fibre, 9 mg chol, 144 mg sodium, 51 mg potassium. % RDI: 2% calcium, 2% iron, 2% vit A, 5% vit C, 3% folate.

Mini Chicken Parmesan Sandwiches

Comfort food like this rarely comes in bite-size portions. On game night, serve a platter of these tiny subs with your favourite beer.

3 **boneless skinless chicken breasts** (about 1 lb/450 g)

⅔ cup **dry bread crumbs**

¼ cup grated **Parmesan cheese**

1 tsp **dried oregano** or basil

2 **eggs**

⅓ cup **all-purpose flour**

½ tsp each **salt** and **pepper**

1 tbsp **vegetable oil**

12 **oval mini-buns** or rolls (about 2 inches/5 cm long), halved horizontally

¾ cup **thick pasta sauce with herbs**

4 thin slices **mozzarella cheese** or provolone cheese (about 4 oz/115 g), cut in thirds

Change It Up

MINI EGGPLANT PARMESAN SANDWICHES

Replace chicken with 1 Japanese eggplant or 2 mini-eggplants, cut into twenty-four ¼-inch (5 mm) thick slices; use 2 rounds per sandwich.

Between plastic wrap, with meat pounder or bottom of heavy pan, pound each chicken breast to ½-inch (1 cm) thickness. Cut each crosswise into 4 strips.

In shallow dish, combine bread crumbs, Parmesan cheese and oregano. In separate shallow dish, beat eggs. In third shallow dish, combine flour, salt and pepper. Press chicken into flour to coat both sides; shake off excess. Dip both sides into egg; press into crumb mixture, turning to coat. *(Make-ahead: Arrange in single layer on waxed paper–lined baking sheet; cover and refrigerate for up to 24 hours.)*

Meanwhile, brush large rimmed baking sheet with oil; heat in 425°F (220°C) oven for 5 minutes. Arrange chicken on pan; bake, turning once, until golden and no longer pink inside, about 15 minutes.

Place buns, cut side up, on large rimless baking sheet. Arrange chicken on bottoms; spread 1 tbsp of the pasta sauce over chicken and top with 1 piece of the cheese. *(Make-ahead: Cover and refrigerate for up to 4 hours.)* Return to oven until cheese is melted and bun tops are lightly toasted, about 5 minutes. Place tops on sandwiches.

165

Makes 12 pieces. PER PIECE: about 233 cal, 17 g pro, 7 g total fat (3 g sat. fat), 24 g carb, 1 g fibre, 63 mg chol, 475 mg sodium. % RDI: 12% calcium, 14% iron, 5% vit A, 3% vit C, 16% folate.

CHAPTER 6

COLD
appetizers

Belgian Endive Spears
With Curried Chicken
Salad (page 173)

167

Chicken & Basil Rolls With Tomato Mayonnaise

These pinwheels look sophisticated but are so easy to make. They're great hot or cold and will wait patiently in the fridge if you make them ahead.

4 **boneless skinless chicken breasts**

2 tbsp **olive oil**

½ tsp each **salt** and **pepper**

1 cup lightly packed **fresh basil leaves**

TOMATO MAYONNAISE:

½ cup **mayonnaise**

2 tbsp **chili sauce** or ketchup

1 tsp **lemon juice**

Pinch **white pepper** or black pepper

1 **plum tomato,** seeded and finely chopped

2 tbsp minced **green onion**

TOMATO MAYONNAISE: In bowl, whisk together mayonnaise, chili sauce, lemon juice and white pepper; stir in tomato and green onion. *(Make-ahead: Cover and refrigerate for up to 24 hours.)*

Between waxed or parchment paper, with meat pounder or bottom of heavy pan, pound each chicken breast evenly to ¼-inch (5 mm) thickness. Brush tops with half of the oil; sprinkle with salt and pepper. Cover with basil leaves; roll up into long cylinders and secure with toothpicks. Place on baking sheets; brush with remaining oil.

Bake in 425°F (220°C) oven until no longer pink inside, about 18 minutes. Let stand for 10 minutes. *(Make-ahead: Wrap and refrigerate for up to 24 hours.)*

Cut into ½-inch (1 cm) thick slices; serve with tomato mayonnaise.

168

Makes about 40 pieces. PER PIECE: about 43 cal, 3 g pro, 3 g total fat (trace sat. fat), trace carb, trace fibre, 10 mg chol, 62 mg sodium. % RDI: 1% iron, 2% vit C, 1% folate.

Fig, Prosciutto & Gorgonzola Salad

Not a blue cheese fan? Try this richly flavoured salad with goat cheese or Brie. The balsamic dressing is delicious on other salads, too.

12 slices **prosciutto** (8 oz/225 g)

24 **dried Mission figs,** halved
(or 12 fresh figs, quartered)

24 cups **mixed baby greens**
(such as arugula, spinach,
mâche and/or romaine)

8 oz (225 g) **Gorgonzola cheese,**
crumbled

½ cup toasted **sliced almonds**

BALSAMIC DRESSING:

¼ cup **balsamic vinegar**

2 tbsp **liquid honey**

1 tsp **Dijon mustard**

Pinch each **salt** and **pepper**

⅓ cup **extra-virgin olive oil**

BALSAMIC DRESSING: In small bowl, whisk together vinegar, honey, mustard, salt and pepper; slowly whisk in oil until combined.

Cut each prosciutto slice lengthwise into 4 strips; wrap each around 1 fig half. Arrange salad greens on serving platter; top with figs, then cheese. Drizzle with dressing; sprinkle with almonds.

169

Change It Up

GRILLED FIG, PROSCIUTTO & GORGONZOLA SALAD

Thread wrapped figs onto metal skewers. Place on greased grill over medium-high heat; close lid and grill, turning once, until prosciutto is slightly crisp, about 5 minutes.

Makes 8 servings. PER SERVING: about 399 cal, 18 g pro, 26 g total fat (9 g sat. fat), 28 g carb, 5 g fibre, 57 mg chol, 1,184 mg sodium, 879 mg potassium. % RDI: 28% calcium, 25% iron, 94% vit A, 55% vit C, 59% folate.

Beef Carpaccio With Arugula

This starter proves how flavour packed a dish can be with just a few quality ingredients. Use a vegetable peeler to shave the cheese into curls.

2 tsp each **mustard seeds** and **black peppercorns**

1½ tsp **fennel seeds**

1 lb (450 g) **beef tenderloin premium oven roast**

½ cup **extra-virgin olive oil**

8 cups **baby arugula**

2 tbsp rinsed drained **capers**

3 oz (85 g) **Parmesan cheese,** shaved

1 tsp **sea salt** or salt

Lemon wedges

170

In spice grinder or mortar and pestle, grind together mustard seeds, peppercorns and fennel seeds until coarsely crushed.

Sprinkle spice mixture on waxed paper; roll beef in spice mixture to coat. In large heavy skillet, heat about 1 tbsp of the oil over medium-high heat until smoking; sear beef all over until spices are just browned, about 45 seconds per side. Refrigerate meat until cold. Wrap tightly in plastic wrap and freeze until firm, about 2½ hours.

Using sharp carving knife, slice beef as thinly as possible. Divide arugula among 8 plates; top with beef. Sprinkle with capers, Parmesan cheese and salt; drizzle with remaining oil. *(Make-ahead: Cover and refrigerate for up to 1 hour.)*

Serve with lemon wedges to squeeze over top.

Makes 8 servings. PER SERVING: about 266 cal, 18 g pro, 20 g total fat (5 g sat. fat), 3 g carb, 1 g fibre, 40 mg chol, 471 mg sodium. % RDI: 20% calcium, 21% iron, 14% vit A, 15% vit C, 27% folate.

Antipasto Platter

Scout farmer's markets for tasty offerings from local cheesemongers and butchers selling house-made salami, prosciutto, pepperoni and other dry sausages. Then add your own marinated olives for an easy hors d'oeuvre.

12 oz (340 g) **sliced deli meats** and/or **kielbasa sausage**

10 oz (280 g) **assorted cheeses,** sliced, cubed or whole

MARINATED OLIVES:

1 cup **mixed brined olives** (such as Niçoise, Kalamata or green)

¼ tsp grated **lemon zest**

¼ tsp each **dried oregano** and **hot pepper flakes**

MARINATED OLIVES: Toss together olives, lemon zest, oregano and hot pepper flakes; let stand for 30 minutes. *(Make-ahead: Refrigerate in airtight container for up to 1 week.)*

Arrange deli meats and cheeses on platter; scatter olives around them.

172

Makes 6 servings. PER SERVING: about 397 cal, 22 g pro, 33 g total fat (14 g sat. fat), 5 g carb, 1 g fibre, 84 mg chol, 1,808 mg sodium. % RDI: 29% calcium, 10% iron, 13% vit A, 3% folate.

Belgian Endive Spears With Curried Chicken Salad

Endive spears are a sturdy base for this tasty filling and add their pleasant bitterness to the mix.

2 **boneless skinless chicken breasts** (12 oz/340 g)

¼ cup **light mayonnaise**

2 tbsp **plain yogurt**

1 tbsp **lime juice** or lemon juice

1 tsp **mild curry paste**

¼ tsp each **salt** and **pepper**

½ cup quartered **red seedless grapes** or green seedless grapes

¼ cup finely chopped **celery**

¼ cup finely chopped **green onion**

2 heads **Belgian endive**

⅓ cup coarsely chopped **unsalted roasted cashews**

In saucepan of simmering water, cover and poach chicken breasts until no longer pink inside, about 12 minutes. Transfer to plate; let cool. Cut into ½-inch (1 cm) cubes.

Meanwhile, in bowl, whisk together mayonnaise, yogurt, lime juice, curry paste, salt and pepper. Stir in chicken, grapes, celery and green onion. *(Make-ahead: Cover and refrigerate for up to 24 hours.)*

Slice about 1 inch (2.5 cm) off root ends of Belgian endives; separate leaves. Stir cashews into chicken salad; mound heaping 1 tbsp on each leaf.

173

Makes about 20 pieces. PER PIECE: about 46 cal, 4 g pro, 2 g total fat (trace sat. fat), 2 g carb, trace fibre, 11 mg chol, 67 mg sodium. % RDI: 1% calcium, 1% iron, 2% vit C, 2% folate.

Gravlax

This Scandinavian cured salmon makes a terrific centrepiece for a cocktail party. It's definitely worth the five days' curing time! Serve with whole grain crackers or pumpernickel rounds and mustard.

1 tbsp **black peppercorns**

⅓ cup **granulated sugar**

¼ cup **pickling salt** or kosher salt

2 lb (900 g) **centre-cut salmon fillet** (skin on)

⅓ cup chopped **fresh dill**

2 tbsp **aquavit,** vodka or gin (optional)

Small dill sprigs

Coarsely crush peppercorns with bottom of heavy pan. Mix with sugar and salt; spread over both sides of salmon. Spread one-third of the chopped dill down centre of large piece of plastic wrap; top with fish, skin side down. Drizzle with aquavit (if using); spread remaining chopped dill over top. Wrap tightly in plastic wrap.

Place on rimmed baking sheet. Place cutting board on fish; weigh down with 2 full 28-oz (796 mL) cans. Refrigerate for 5 days, turning fish daily.

Unwrap fish. Using paper towel, brush off most of the dill. (*Make-ahead: Wrap in plastic wrap; refrigerate for up to 5 days.*)

Slice thinly on 45-degree angle. Garnish with dill sprigs.

175

Makes about 50 pieces. PER PIECE: about 35 cal, 3 g pro, 2 g total fat (trace sat. fat), 1 g carb, 0 g fibre, 10 mg chol, 369 mg sodium. % RDI: 1% iron, 2% vit C, 2% folate.

Mushroom Maki Rolls

Serve these vegetarian rolls with pickled ginger and sushi soy sauce, which is milder and sweeter than regular soy sauce. Wet your hands before spreading the sushi rice to keep it from sticking to your fingers.

2 tsp each **vegetable oil** and **sesame oil**

1¼ lb (565 g) **shiitake mushrooms,** stemmed and halved if large

2 cloves **garlic,** minced

1 tbsp **mirin** or sherry

1 tbsp **sodium-reduced soy sauce** or sushi soy sauce

1 pkg (3½ oz/100 g) **enoki mushrooms,** trimmed

6 sheets **roasted nori**

3 **green onions,** thinly sliced lengthwise

1 cup **watercress,** trimmed

SUSHI RICE:

1 cup **sushi rice,** rinsed (see How-To, below)

3 tbsp **unseasoned rice vinegar**

4 tsp **granulated sugar**

¾ tsp **salt**

176

How-To

RINSING SUSHI RICE

Rice dust tends to coat sushi rice, which can make it sticky when cooked. To remove it, in fine sieve, rinse rice under cold running water, stirring vigorously until water runs clear. Drain well.

SUSHI RICE: In saucepan, bring rice and 1¼ cups cold water to boil; stir once. Cover and simmer over low heat for 13 minutes. Remove from heat. Uncover and drape tea towel over pan; replace lid. Let stand for 10 minutes. Transfer to large glass baking dish or bowl. Meanwhile, in glass measure, microwave vinegar, sugar and salt at high until hot, 25 seconds. Stir just until sugar dissolves; let cool completely. Drizzle over rice; gently toss with wooden spoon to coat grains. To cool rice quickly, spread over surface of baking dish; loosely cover with tea towel and let cool completely at room temperature, about 30 minutes. Do not refrigerate.

Meanwhile, in skillet, heat vegetable and sesame oils over medium-high heat; sauté shiitakes and garlic until softened, 5 minutes. Stir in mirin and soy sauce; cook until no liquid remains, 2 minutes. Scrape into bowl; let cool for 15 minutes. *(Make-ahead: Cover and refrigerate for up to 12 hours.)*

Separate enokis into strands. For each roll, place 1 nori sheet, shiny side down and with long edge closest, on sushi rolling mat. Leaving ½-inch (1 cm) border at long edges, spread ½ cup rice evenly over nori. Lay one-sixth of the shiitake mixture 2 inches (5 cm) from closest long edge; top with one-sixth each of the enokis, onions and watercress. Starting at closest edge of mat, roll up firmly. *(Make-ahead: Wrap in paper towels; set aside for up to 2 hours.)*

Trim ends; cut each roll into 8 slices, wiping knife with wet cloth between cuts.

Makes 48 pieces. PER PIECE: about 23 cal, 1 g pro, trace total fat (0 g sat. fat), 4 g carb, trace fibre, 0 mg chol, 52 mg sodium. % RDI: 1% iron, 1% vit A, 2% vit C, 2% folate.

Swiss Chicken Crêpes

This combination of cheese and smoked chicken is easy to whip up on a whim. Mustard helps hold the spirals together, but you can use toothpicks if you want to be doubly sure.

16 slices **deli smoked chicken**
  (8 oz/225 g)

16 thin slices **Swiss cheese**
  (8 oz/225 g)

3 tbsp **Dijon mustard**

BEST BASIC CRÊPES:

1⅓ cups **all-purpose flour**

¼ tsp **salt**

4 **eggs**

1½ cups **milk**

¼ cup **butter,** melted

BEST BASIC CRÊPES: In bowl, whisk flour with salt. Whisk together eggs, milk and 2 tbsp of the butter; pour over dry ingredients and whisk until smooth. Strain into bowl. Cover and refrigerate for 1 hour. *(Make-ahead: Refrigerate for up to 24 hours.)*

Heat 8-inch (20 cm) crêpe pan or nonstick skillet over medium heat. Brush pan with some of the remaining butter. Pour scant ¼ cup batter into centre of pan, swirling to coat; cook, turning once, until golden, about 1 minute. Transfer to plate. Repeat to make 16 crêpes. *(Make-ahead: Layer between waxed paper and wrap in plastic wrap; refrigerate for up to 24 hours or freeze in airtight container for up to 1 month. Thaw in refrigerator.)*

On each crêpe, place 1 slice of the chicken, then 1 slice of the cheese; spread each with about ½ tsp of the mustard. Roll up tightly. Wrap each in plastic wrap and refrigerate for 1 hour. *(Make-ahead: Refrigerate for up to 24 hours.)*

Trim ends; cut crêpes crosswise into quarters; stand each upright or stack on platter.

177

Makes 64 pieces. PER PIECE: about 41 cal, 3 g pro, 2 g total fat (1 g sat. fat), 3 g carb, trace fibre, 19 mg chol, 58 mg sodium, 26 mg potassium. % RDI: 4% calcium, 1% iron, 2% vit A, 3% folate.

Classic Shrimp Cocktail

Take shrimp cocktail on a trip around the world with these quick and easy cocktail sauce variations. It sounds a little crazy, but the pineapple version is incredibly delicious!

2 lb (900 g) **raw large shrimp,** peeled and deveined

COCKTAIL SAUCE:

½ cup **ketchup**

2 tbsp **prepared horseradish**

2 tbsp **lemon juice**

2 tsp **Worcestershire sauce**

¼ tsp **hot pepper sauce**

In pot of boiling salted water, cook shrimp until pink and opaque, about 3 minutes. Drain and chill under cold water; drain and pat dry. Arrange on platter.

COCKTAIL SAUCE: Stir together ketchup, horseradish, lemon juice, Worcestershire sauce and hot pepper sauce until combined. Serve with shrimp for dipping.

178

Change It Up

THAI SHRIMP COCKTAIL

Omit Cocktail Sauce. Stir together ½ cup ketchup; 2 tbsp lime juice; 1 tbsp prepared horseradish; 1 tsp minced red finger hot pepper; 1 tsp fish sauce or soy sauce; 1 green onion, minced; and ½ tsp red Thai curry paste.

GREEN OLIVE & PAPRIKA SHRIMP COCKTAIL

Omit Cocktail Sauce. Stir together ½ cup ketchup, 2 tbsp finely chopped green olives, 2 tbsp lemon juice, 1 tbsp prepared horseradish, 2 tsp Worcestershire sauce and 1 tsp smoked paprika.

MEDITERRANEAN SHRIMP COCKTAIL

Omit Cocktail Sauce. Stir together ½ cup ketchup; 2 tbsp chopped rinsed drained capers; 1 tsp grated lemon zest; 2 tbsp lemon juice; 1 tbsp each chopped fresh parsley, mayonnaise and prepared horseradish; 2 tsp Worcestershire sauce; and 1 clove garlic, minced.

PINEAPPLE SHRIMP COCKTAIL

Omit Cocktail Sauce. Stir together ½ cup ketchup, ⅓ cup drained canned crushed pineapple, 1 tbsp prepared horseradish, ¼ tsp hot pepper sauce and pinch ground allspice.

Makes 24 pieces. PER PIECE: about 36 cal, 6 g pro, 1 g total fat (trace sat. fat), 2 g carb, trace fibre, 43 mg chol, 104 mg sodium. % RDI: 2% calcium, 5% iron, 2% vit A, 3% vit C, 2% folate.

Avocado Shrimp Brochettes

Colourful and fresh, these skewers are inspired by the citrusy seafood salads of Thailand and Central America. For a real hit of spiciness, use a Thai bird's-eye pepper; for a milder taste, use a seeded jalapeño pepper.

24 **raw large shrimp** (12 oz/340 g), peeled and deveined

¼ cup **lime juice**

3 tbsp finely chopped **red onion**

2 tsp **fish sauce** (or ½ tsp salt)

1½ tsp grated **fresh ginger**

2 tbsp minced **fresh cilantro**

2 tbsp minced **fresh mint** or basil (optional)

1 tbsp **peanut oil** or olive oil

1 tsp minced **hot pepper**

2 **avocados**

1 tbsp finely chopped **unsalted roasted peanuts**

In saucepan of boiling salted water, cook shrimp until pink and opaque, about 3 minutes. Drain and chill under cold water; drain and pat dry.

Toss together shrimp, lime juice, red onion, fish sauce and ginger; cover and refrigerate for 1 hour. Add cilantro, mint (if using), oil and hot pepper, tossing to coat.

Pit, peel and cut each avocado into twenty-four 1-inch (2.5 cm) cubes. Thread 1 avocado cube and 1 shrimp onto each of 24 cocktail skewers. Arrange on serving plate; drizzle with any juices from bowl. Sprinkle with peanuts.

179

Makes 24 pieces. PER PIECE: about 41 cal, 2 g pro, 3 g total fat (1 g sat. fat), 2 g carb, trace fibre, 11 mg chol, 55 mg sodium. % RDI: 3% iron, 2% vit A, 3% vit C, 5% folate.

Scallop Seviche

Use a large pot for blanching scallops to ensure that the water remains at the boiling point and the scallops get cooked through in the shortest amount of time.

8 oz (225 g) **bay scallops** (or sea scallops, cut in ½-inch/1 cm cubes)

1 tbsp **extra-virgin olive oil**

¼ cup **lime juice**

½ tsp **salt**

¼ tsp **hot pepper flakes**

½ cup diced seeded **English cucumber**

2 tbsp each finely diced **sweet red pepper** and **sweet yellow pepper**

2 tbsp chopped **fresh mint** or cilantro

In large saucepan of boiling water, cook scallops just until firm, about 1 minute; drain. Transfer to bowl and toss with oil; let cool. Drain. *(Make-ahead: Cover and refrigerate for up to 8 hours.)*

Stir in lime juice, salt and hot pepper flakes. Cover and refrigerate for 15 minutes. *(Make-ahead: Refrigerate for up to 3 hours.)*

Mix in cucumber, red and yellow peppers, and mint. To serve, divide among small bowls or Chinese soup spoons.

181

Makes 8 servings. PER SERVING: about 44 cal, 5 g pro, 2 g total fat (trace sat. fat), 2 g carb, trace fibre, 9 mg chol, 191 mg sodium. % RDI: 1% calcium, 1% iron, 3% vit A, 17% vit C, 2% folate.

Tuna Tartare

Sushi-grade tuna – bought fresh from your local fish market – is the only way to ensure the quality and taste of this dish. It's worth the splurge.

12 oz (340 g) **fresh tuna fillet,** diced

¼ cup finely diced **red onion**

2 tbsp minced **fresh parsley**

1 tbsp minced drained **capers**

2 tsp **Worcestershire sauce**

2 tsp **Dijon mustard**

1 tsp **lemon juice**

Pinch each **salt** and **pepper**

In bowl, stir together tuna, red onion, parsley, capers, Worcestershire sauce, mustard, lemon juice, salt and pepper. Serve immediately.

182

Makes about 1 cup, or 24 servings. PER SERVING: about 22 cal, 3 g pro, 1 g total fat (trace sat. fat), trace carb, trace fibre, 5 mg chol, 37 mg sodium, 44 mg potassium. % RDI: 1% iron, 10% vit A, 2% vit C.

Poached Shrimp & Crudités With Basil Aïoli

Here's a tasty combined approach to shrimp cocktail and veggies with dip. The shrimp, vegetables and aïoli can all be made ahead, wrapped separately and assembled just before the party.

1 **onion,** sliced

Half **lemon,** sliced

3 **bay leaves**

3 stalks **fresh parsley**

1 tbsp **coriander seeds**

1 tsp **black peppercorns**

½ tsp **salt**

2 lb (900 g) **raw large shrimp,** peeled and deveined

8 oz (225 g) each **asparagus, rapini** (or broccolini), **green beans, yellow beans, radishes** and **cherry tomatoes**

1 **English cucumber** (12 inches/ 30 cm)

1 **jicama** (8 oz/225 g)

Basil Aïoli (page 18)

In saucepan, bring 6 cups water to boil; add onion, lemon, bay leaves, parsley, coriander seeds, peppercorns and salt. Reduce heat, cover and simmer for 15 minutes. Strain into clean saucepan; bring to boil. Cook shrimp until pink and opaque, about 3 minutes. Drain and chill under cold water; drain and pat dry.

Bring large saucepan of salted water to boil. One at a time, place asparagus, rapini, green beans, yellow beans, radishes and tomatoes in large sieve; plunge into boiling water and cook just until tender-crisp, 2 to 3 minutes each. Plunge into ice water to stop cooking. Drain and arrange on paper towel–lined trays. *(Make-ahead: Cover shrimp and vegetables separately with plastic wrap and refrigerate for up to 6 hours.)*

Cut cucumber lengthwise into quarters; cut each into 8 long pieces. Peel and slice jicama. Arrange all vegetables on platter along with shrimp; serve with basil aïoli.

183

Makes 20 servings. PER SERVING: about 210 cal, 9 g pro, 17 g total fat (3 g sat. fat), 6 g carb, 2 g fibre, 58 mg chol, 215 mg sodium, 266 mg potassium. % RDI: 5% calcium, 12% iron, 9% vit A, 18% vit C, 18% folate.

Rice Paper Lobster Rolls

Cooking a fresh lobster ensures great taste. If you are short on time, many fish markets will cook it for you.

1 **cooked lobster** (1 lb/450 g), shelled (see How-To, page 83)

12 large **fresh mint leaves,** chopped

½ cup thinly sliced **sweet red pepper**

½ cup thinly sliced seeded halved **cucumber**

¼ cup thinly sliced peeled **firm ripe mango**

1 tbsp finely chopped **unsalted roasted peanuts**

2 tsp **lime juice**

1 tsp each **fish sauce** and **vegetable oil**

½ tsp finely minced **finger hot pepper** or jalapeño pepper

12 **rice paper wrappers** (9 inches/ 23 cm)

¾ cup chopped **romaine lettuce** (4 leaves)

DIPPING SAUCE:

¼ cup **sweet Thai chili sauce**

2 tbsp **unseasoned rice vinegar**

1 tsp **fish sauce**

DIPPING SAUCE: Stir together chili sauce, vinegar, 2 tbsp water and fish sauce; set aside.

Cut lobster meat into small pieces. In bowl, stir together lobster, mint, red pepper, cucumber, mango, peanuts, lime juice, fish sauce, oil and hot pepper.

Fill shallow dish with lukewarm water; soak rice paper wrappers, 1 at a time, until pliable, 30 to 60 seconds. Transfer to tea towel; pat dry.

Place 4 tsp lobster mixture and 1 tbsp lettuce at bottom of each wrapper. Fold sides over filling; tightly roll up. *(Make-ahead: Place on plastic wrap-lined plate and cover with damp towel; overwrap with plastic wrap and refrigerate for up to 4 hours.)*

Cut rolls in half. Serve with dipping sauce.

184

Makes 24 pieces. PER PIECE: about 28 cal, 2 g pro, 1 g total fat (trace sat. fat), 4 g carb, trace fibre, 4 mg chol, 102 mg sodium, 40 mg potassium. % RDI: 1% calcium, 1% iron, 2% vit A, 8% vit C, 4% folate.

Snow Pea Shrimp With Lemon Aïoli

Snow peas add a fresh crunch to every bite of tender shrimp, which is made even more delicious by the garlicky, citrusy mayonnaise.

20 **raw large shrimp** (about 12 oz/340 g), peeled and deveined

Half **lemon**

20 large **snow peas** (12 oz/ 340 g), trimmed

LEMON AÏOLI:

½ cup **light mayonnaise**

1 small clove **garlic,** minced

2 tsp grated **lemon zest**

2 tsp **lemon juice**

Pinch each **salt** and **pepper**

186

Fill large saucepan with enough water to come 1 inch (2.5 cm) up side; cover and bring to boil. Reduce heat to medium-low. Arrange shrimp in single layer in steamer basket. Cut lemon into quarters; squeeze over shrimp. Nestle squeezed lemon quarters in basket among shrimp; cover and steam until shrimp are pink and opaque, about 6 minutes. Transfer to plate; let cool. *(Make-ahead: Cover and refrigerate for up to 24 hours.)*

Meanwhile, in saucepan of boiling salted water, blanch snow peas for 1 minute. Drain and chill in cold water; drain and pat dry.

Wrap 1 snow pea around each shrimp; skewer with toothpick. *(Make-ahead: Cover and refrigerate for up to 4 hours.)*

LEMON AÏOLI: Stir together mayonnaise, garlic, lemon zest, lemon juice, salt and pepper. *(Make-ahead: Cover and refrigerate for up to 24 hours.)*

Serve shrimp with lemon aïoli for dipping.

Makes 20 pieces. PER PIECE: about 39 cal, 3 g pro, 2 g total fat (trace sat. fat), 2 g carb, trace fibre, 21 mg chol, 63 mg sodium. % RDI: 1% calcium, 4% iron, 1% vit A, 15% vit C, 3% folate.

Fresh Rolls With Spicy Almond Dipping Sauce

This Vietnamese favourite is easy to make as a main course or an appetizer. Look for angel hair–size rice vermicelli and rice paper wrappers in the Asian section of the grocery store.

4 oz (115 g) **fine rice stick vermicelli**

1 tsp **sesame oil**

12 **rice paper wrappers** (9 inches/23 cm)

36 **cooked large shrimp**

3 cups thinly sliced **leaf lettuce**

Half each **sweet red pepper** and **sweet yellow pepper,** thinly sliced

1 piece (4 inches/10 cm) **English cucumber,** cut in thin strips

Half **mango,** peeled and thinly sliced

1 cup each **fresh mint leaves** and **fresh cilantro leaves**

SPICY ALMOND DIPPING SAUCE:

¼ cup **crunchy natural almond butter**

¼ cup **hoisin sauce**

2 tbsp each **seasoned rice vinegar** and **sodium-reduced soy sauce**

1 tbsp **sriracha** or other Asian hot sauce

SPICY ALMOND DIPPING SAUCE: Stir together almond butter, hoisin sauce, rice vinegar, soy sauce, sriracha and 3 tbsp water; set aside.

Break vermicelli into thirds; place in bowl. Pour boiling water over top; soak until tender, about 3 minutes. Drain and toss with sesame oil; let cool.

Fill shallow bowl with warm water. Soak 1 rice paper wrapper in water until softened and pliable, about 30 seconds. Transfer to tea towel; pat dry.

Along bottom third of wrapper, place 3 shrimp. Top with scant ¼ cup of the vermicelli, ¼ cup of the lettuce and a few pieces each of the red pepper, yellow pepper, cucumber and mango. Top with 2 or 3 leaves each of the mint and cilantro.

From filled side, roll wrapper over filling. Fold sides over and tightly roll up. Place, seam side down, on tray; cover with damp towel. Repeat with remaining ingredients to make 12 rolls.

Cut rolls diagonally in half. Serve with sauce.

187

Makes 24 pieces. PER PIECE: about 76 cal, 3 g pro, 2 g total fat (trace sat. fat), 11 g carb, 1 g fibre, 16 mg chol, 176 mg sodium, 93 mg potassium. % RDI: 2% calcium, 7% iron, 7% vit A, 20% vit C, 5% folate.

Smoked Salmon Bites With Dill Caper Cream

These elegant bites look lovely as they are, but you can dress them up even more by topping them with fish roe or tiny dill sprigs.

26 drained **capers**

¼ cup **light mayonnaise**

2 tsp finely chopped **fresh dill** (or ½ tsp dried dillweed)

1 tsp **lemon juice**

¼ tsp **pepper**

5 thin slices **smoked salmon**

1 piece (3 inches/8 cm) **English cucumber**

20 **Toast Cups** (page 131)

Remove 20 capers and set aside. Coarsely chop remaining capers; place in small bowl. Stir in mayonnaise, dill, lemon juice and pepper.

Cut salmon into 1½- x ½-inch (4 x 1 cm) strips; roll into rosettes. Quarter cucumber lengthwise; thinly slice crosswise. *(Make-ahead: Cover and refrigerate salmon, cucumber, capers and mayonnaise mixture separately for up to 8 hours.)*

Spoon ½ tsp mayonnaise mixture into each toast cup. Tuck 1 salmon rosette and 2 cucumber slices in each; garnish each with 1 of the reserved capers.

189

Makes about 20 pieces. PER PIECE: about 39 cal, 1 g pro, 2 g total fat (trace sat. fat), 4 g carb, trace fibre, 2 mg chol, 94 mg sodium, 21 mg potassium. % RDI: 1% calcium, 2% iron, 4% folate.

Classic Devilled Eggs

Devilled eggs are a guaranteed crowd-pleaser. Stick with the classic filling or spice things up with one of the fantastic variations.

12 **eggs**

FILLING:

¼ cup **mayonnaise**

3 tbsp **sour cream**

¼ tsp **dry mustard**

¼ tsp each **salt** and **pepper**

GARNISH:

¼ tsp **sweet paprika**

Arrange eggs in single layer in large deep saucepan; pour in enough cold water to come at least 1 inch (2.5 cm) above eggs. Cover and bring to boil over high heat. Immediately remove from heat; let stand, covered, for 20 minutes. Drain and chill under cold water. *(Make-ahead: Refrigerate in airtight container for up to 2 days.)*

Peel off shells. Cut eggs in half lengthwise; scoop yolks into bowl. Set whites on serving platter; cover and set aside.

FILLING: Using fork, mash together egg yolks, mayonnaise, sour cream, mustard, salt and pepper. Spoon into pastry bag fitted with 1-inch (2.5 cm) star tip; pipe into egg whites. (Alternatively, spoon filling into whites.)

GARNISH: Sprinkle with paprika.

Change It Up

SMOKED SALMON DEVILLED EGGS

Omit Filling and Garnish. Mash egg yolks, ⅓ cup mayonnaise, 2 tbsp prepared horseradish, and ¼ tsp each salt and pepper. Garnish each with smoked salmon and 1 tbsp chopped fresh chives.

MEXICAN-STYLE DEVILLED EGGS

Omit Filling and Garnish. Mash egg yolks, ⅓ cup sour cream, 3 tbsp mayonnaise, ½ tsp chili powder, and ¼ tsp each salt and pepper. Garnish each with 1 pickled jalapeño pepper ring, rinsed and patted dry; and 1 leaf fresh cilantro.

WESTERN-STYLE DEVILLED EGGS

Omit Filling and Garnish. Mash egg yolks; ⅓ cup mayonnaise; ⅓ cup finely diced sweet green pepper; 1 green onion, minced; and ¼ tsp each salt and pepper. Garnish each with crumbled cooked bacon.

Makes 24 pieces. PER PIECE: about 56 cal, 3 g pro, 5 g total fat (1 g sat. fat), trace carb, 0 g fibre, 95 mg chol, 68 mg sodium. % RDI: 1% calcium, 2% iron, 4% vit A, 6% folate.

Camembert & Fig Skewers With Balsamic Sauce

Sweet and salty, these skewers have just the right amount of tang from the vinegar. They're a pretty take on the typical cheese-and-fruit combo.

8 oz (225 g) cold **Camembert cheese** or Brie cheese

1 cup **orange juice**

½ cup **balsamic vinegar**

12 **dried figs,** quartered

2 tsp **granulated sugar**

Cut cheese into forty-eight 1- x ½-inch (2.5 x 1 cm) pieces; thread 1 piece onto each of 48 skewers. Arrange on waxed paper–lined baking sheets. Cover and set aside in refrigerator.

In small saucepan, heat orange juice and balsamic vinegar over medium-high heat. Add figs; simmer until slightly softened, about 5 minutes. Using slotted spoon, transfer figs to sieve set over bowl.

Bring orange juice mixture to boil; reduce heat and simmer until reduced to ½ cup, 15 to 20 minutes. Stir in sugar. Transfer to serving bowl; let cool. *(Make-ahead: Cover and refrigerate skewers, figs and sauce for up to 6 hours.)*

191

Thread fig pieces onto skewers alongside cheese. Serve with sauce for dipping.

Makes 48 pieces. PER PIECE: about 27 cal, 1 g pro, 1 g total fat (1 g sat. fat), 3 g carb, trace fibre, 3 mg chol, 40 mg sodium. % RDI: 2% calcium, 1% iron, 1% vit A, 3% vit C, 2% folate.

Marinated Roasted Peppers & Feta

Summery Mediterranean-inspired feta cubes are best served with sliced baguette to soak up the flavourful olive oil. Crushing the fresh herbs releases their aromas.

½ cup chopped drained **jarred roasted red peppers**

½ cup **extra-virgin olive oil**

4 sprigs each **fresh oregano** and **fresh thyme,** crushed

¼ tsp **hot pepper flakes**

10 oz (280 g) **feta cheese,** cubed

In shallow dish, stir together red peppers, oil, oregano, thyme and hot pepper flakes; gently stir in feta cheese. Cover and refrigerate for 2 hours. *(Make-ahead: Refrigerate for up to 24 hours.)*

192

Makes 8 to 12 servings. PER EACH OF 12 SERVINGS: about 145 cal, 4 g pro, 14 g total fat (5 g sat. fat), 2 g carb, trace fibre, 22 mg chol, 277 mg sodium, 31 mg potassium. % RDI: 11% calcium, 3% iron, 6% vit A, 17% vit C, 5% folate.

Eggplant Rolls With Goat Cheese & Sun-Dried Tomatoes

Oil-packed or soaked dry-packed sun-dried tomatoes work equally well.

2 large **eggplants** (about 1 lb/ 450 g each)

1½ tsp **salt**

3 tbsp **extra-virgin olive oil**

10 oz (280 g) **soft goat cheese**

½ cup chopped **sun-dried tomatoes**

¼ cup chopped **fresh basil** or parsley

¼ cup **whipping cream** (35%)

½ tsp **pepper**

1 tbsp **balsamic vinegar**

194

Cut eggplants lengthwise into ¼-inch (5 mm) thick slices, discarding outermost slices with skin. Sprinkle all over with salt; arrange in single layer on baking sheets. Place 1 of the sheets on top of the other; top with another baking sheet. Weigh down with heavy cans; let stand for 30 minutes. Pat eggplant dry.

Brush both sides of eggplant with oil; bake on parchment paper–lined baking sheets in 400°F (200°C) oven, turning once, until golden and softened, about 25 minutes. Let cool.

Meanwhile, in bowl, mash together goat cheese, tomatoes, basil, cream and pepper; set aside.

Brush 1 side of eggplant with vinegar; cut each slice in half crosswise. Place scant 1 tbsp filling at cut end of each; roll up to enclose stuffing. Skewer rolls with toothpicks; arrange on platter. Serve at room temperature or chilled. *(Make-ahead: Cover and refrigerate for up to 24 hours.)*

Makes about 40 pieces. PER PIECE: about 43 cal, 2 g pro, 3 g total fat (2 g sat. fat), 3 g carb, 1 g fibre, 5 mg chol, 87 mg sodium, 59 mg potassium. % RDI: 1% calcium, 2% iron, 3% vit A, 2% vit C, 2% folate.

Roasted Garlic & Blue Cheese Olives

A burst of savoury flavour is nestled inside each olive. An assertive Danish blue cheese is best – and most budget-friendly. If you can't find pitted green olives, remove the pimiento from stuffed green olives.

1 head **garlic**

½ tsp **extra-virgin olive oil**

½ cup crumbled **blue cheese** (2 oz/55 g), softened

¼ tsp **pepper**

36 pitted large **green olives**

Trim top off garlic to expose cloves. Place on small square of foil and drizzle with oil; seal to form package. Roast in 375°F (190°C) oven until tender, 50 to 60 minutes. Let cool enough to handle; squeeze pulp into bowl. Add blue cheese and pepper; mash until blended.

Rinse olives; pat dry. Spoon cheese mixture into piping bag fitted with large round tip or resealable plastic bag with corner snipped off; pipe into olives. *(Make-ahead: Cover and refrigerate for up to 3 days.)*

195

Makes 36 pieces. PER PIECE: about 15 cal, 1 g pro, 1 g total fat (trace sat. fat), 1 g carb, trace fibre, 1 mg chol, 95 mg sodium, 11 mg potassium. % RDI: 1% calcium, 1% vit A.

Sushi Bars

These beautiful stacked sushi bars are a nice change from traditional rolls. Sushi rice is easy to find in Asian stores and many supermarkets.

1¼ cups **sushi rice,** rinsed
(see How-To, page 176)

3 tbsp **unseasoned rice vinegar**

1 tsp **salt**

¼ cup **light mayonnaise**

1 tsp **wasabi powder**

1 tsp **lemon juice**

4 sheets **roasted nori**

1 jar (313 mL) **roasted red peppers,** drained

1 bunch **arugula**

Pickled ginger (optional)

196

In saucepan, bring 1½ cups water and rice to boil. Reduce heat to low; cover and cook until rice is tender and water is absorbed, about 25 minutes. With fork, toss in vinegar and salt; let cool completely. *(Make-ahead: Cover and refrigerate for up to 12 hours.)*

Stir together mayonnaise, wasabi powder and lemon juice; set aside.

Place 1 sheet of the nori, shiny side down, on work surface. With damp fingers, press 1 cup of the rice onto nori, spreading evenly to edges. Lay one-third of the roasted red peppers on top of rice; top with one-third of the arugula leaves. Spread with 1 tbsp of the mayonnaise mixture. Top with second sheet of nori, shiny side down, and gently press down. Repeat layers twice to create 3 layers, ending with final sheet of nori, shiny side up. Wrap well in plastic wrap and refrigerate for 2 hours. *(Make-ahead: Refrigerate for up to 6 hours.)*

Using sharp knife, cut into 1-inch (2.5 cm) squares, wiping knife with wet cloth between cuts. Top each square with small piece of pickled ginger (if using).

Makes 56 pieces. PER PIECE: about 22 cal, trace pro, trace total fat (0 g sat. fat), 4 g carb, trace fibre, 0 mg chol, 50 mg sodium. % RDI: 1% iron, 2% vit A, 8% vit C, 2% folate.

Stuffed Grape Leaves

This type of stuffed grape leaf is often known by the Greek name *dolma* – or *dolmades* when there's a plateful.

⅓ cup **extra-virgin olive oil**

⅓ cup **pine nuts**

2 **onions,** chopped

2 cloves **garlic,** minced

1 cup **long-grain rice**

2 **tomatoes,** peeled, seeded and finely chopped

½ cup chopped **fresh parsley**

½ cup chopped **fresh mint** (or 2 tbsp dried)

½ cup **lemon juice**

⅓ cup **dried currants** or raisins

1¼ tsp each **salt** and **cinnamon**

1 tsp **granulated sugar**

½ tsp **pepper**

¼ tsp **ground cloves**

1 jar (500 mL) **grape leaves**

In skillet, heat 2 tbsp of the oil over medium-high heat; sauté pine nuts until slightly darkened, about 2 minutes. Add onions and garlic; cook, stirring occasionally, until softened, about 3 minutes.

In large bowl, combine onion mixture, rice, tomatoes, parsley, mint, half of the lemon juice, the currants, salt, cinnamon, sugar, pepper and cloves; set aside.

Rinse grape leaves under cold running water. In large pot of boiling water, blanch, in 2 batches, for 3 minutes. Chill under cold running water; drain. Pat leaves dry; cut off stems.

Line shallow Dutch oven with any broken leaves or 5 whole leaves. Lay 1 grape leaf, shiny side down, on work surface; place rounded 1 tbsp of the rice mixture on bottom third of leaf; fold over sides and roll up snugly but not as tightly as possible (filling will expand). Repeat with remaining grape leaves and rice mixture.

Place rolls, touching and seam side down, in Dutch oven. Pour remaining olive oil and lemon juice, and 2 cups water over top; cover rolls with inverted heatproof plate. Cover with lid and bring to boil; reduce heat and simmer for 45 minutes. Uncover and cook until no liquid remains, about 5 minutes. Let cool for 30 minutes. *(Make-ahead: Refrigerate in airtight container for up to 3 days.)*

197

Makes about 60 pieces. PER PIECE: about 34 cal, 1 g pro, 2 g total fat (trace sat. fat), 4 g carb, 1 g fibre, 0 mg chol, 163 mg sodium. % RDI: 2% calcium, 2% iron, 1% vit A, 3% vit C, 3% folate.

drinks & snacks

From left: Curried Nuts & Bolts
(page 234) and Ginger Beer
Shandy (page 207)

199

Original Champagne Cocktail

For an even more elegant cocktail (touched with romance), use pink Champagne, as Deborah Kerr and Cary Grant did in the movie *An Affair to Remember.*

1 **sugar cube**

Dash **Angostura bitters**

5 oz (⅔ cup) chilled **Champagne**

Lemon twist

Place sugar cube in champagne glass; soak with bitters. Top with Champagne.

Garnish with lemon twist.

200

How-To

CUTTING A CITRUS TWIST

Sometimes a drink needs a little extra something to dress it up. This Champagne Cocktail gets a boost from a freshly cut lemon twist added right before serving. The easiest way to make a twist is with a gadget called a channel knife. Use it to cut a 3-inch (8 cm) strip of zest; if you don't have a channel knife, use a very sharp small paring knife, avoiding the white pith below the zest. Tie in a little knot and drop into cocktail. Or wrap around a wooden spoon handle or chopstick to make a spiral; anchor one end of the spiral over the rim of the glass and let the rest flavour the drink.

Makes 1 serving. PER SERVING: about 115 cal, trace pro, 0 g total fat (0 g sat. fat), 4 g carb, 0 g fibre, 0 mg chol, 8 mg sodium, 125 mg potassium. % RDI: 1% calcium, 4% iron.

Black Velvet

This cocktail has a rich, malty flavour that beer drinkers will love. It's wonderful served with oysters or other savoury appetizers.

2 oz (¼ cup) **stout**

2 oz (¼ cup) chilled **Champagne**

Pour stout into champagne glass; let settle before adding Champagne to prevent overflow.

Gently pour Champagne down side of glass to combine and create small head.

202

How-To

MAKING THE PERFECT CHAMPAGNE COCKTAILS

A mid-priced Champagne or sparkling wine is best for mixing. Spanish Cava, Italian Prosecco and good-quality Canadian sparklers are reasonable and tasty options. Since Champagne cocktails tend to be on the sweet side, choose a dry (Brut) Champagne or sparkling wine. Chill it before using and add to the glass last. Pour it slowly over the other ingredients to avoid overflowing bubbles. Stirring isn't usually necessary for these drinks; if you must, stir slowly and gently, and enjoy immediately – before the bubbles disappear.

Makes 1 serving. PER SERVING: about 64 cal, trace pro, 0 g total fat (0 g sat. fat), 3 g carb, 0 g fibre, 0 mg chol, 6 mg sodium, 60 mg potassium. % RDI: 1% calcium, 1% iron, 2% folate.

French 75

This tart and tangy cocktail is very elegant served with light appetizers. Simple syrup is used in cocktails because it blends better than sugar.

Ice cubes

2 oz (¼ cup) **gin**

1 oz (2 tbsp) **lemon juice**

1 tbsp **Simple Syrup** (below)

4 oz (½ cup) chilled **Champagne,** Canadian sparkling wine, prosecco or cava

Fill cocktail shaker with ice. Add gin, lemon juice and simple syrup; shake to blend and chill.

Strain into champagne glasses; top each with Champagne.

Make Your Own

SIMPLE SYRUP

In measuring cup, whisk together ½ cup each granulated sugar and boiling water until clear and sugar is dissolved. **Makes ¾ cup.**

203

Makes 2 servings. PER SERVING: about 129 cal, trace pro, 0 g total fat (0 g sat. fat), 8 g carb, trace fibre, 0 mg chol, 4 mg sodium, 65 mg potassium. % RDI: 1% calcium, 2% iron, 12% vit C, 1% folate.

Cava Sangria

This Spanish punch is a blend of wine, spirits and fruit. This recipe uses sparkling wine, but we've included a classic red wine variation as well. When nectarines and peaches are in season, add them to the mix.

1 each **lemon, lime** and **orange**

1 **apple** or peach

⅓ cup **granulated sugar**

Pinch **salt**

¼ cup **brandy**

1 bottle (750 mL) **cava** or sparkling dry white wine

2 cups **ice cubes**

Quarter lemon, lime, orange and apple; seed and thinly slice.

Placed sliced fruit in pitcher; stir in sugar and salt. Let stand for 1 hour. *(Make-ahead: Cover and refrigerate for up to 2 days.)*

Add brandy. Slightly mash fruit. Stir in cava and ice. Serve immediately.

Change It Up

205

CLASSIC SANGRIA

Substitute full-bodied red wine for cava.

Makes 6 servings. PER SERVING: about 154 cal, trace pro, 0 g total fat (0 g sat. fat), 14 g carb, 0 g fibre, 0 mg chol, 7 mg sodium. % RDI: 1% calcium, 3% iron, 10% vit C, 1% folate.

Kir Royale

This black currant Champagne cocktail is perfect for brunch or as an aperitif.

1 tbsp **crème de cassis**

5 oz (⅔ cup) chilled **Champagne**

Pour crème de cassis into champagne glass; top with Champagne.

Change It Up

ICE WINE ROYALE
Substitute Vidal or Riesling icewine for crème de cassis.

FRAMBOISE ROYALE
Substitute Chambord or other raspberry liqueur for crème de cassis.

206

Makes 1 serving. PER SERVING: about 136 cal, trace pro, 0 g total fat (0 g sat. fat), 7 g carb, 0 g fibre, 0 mg chol, 7 mg sodium, 114 mg potassium. % RDI: 1% calcium, 4% iron.

Ginger Beer Shandy

Created by British colonists in the 19th century, the shandy is a popular and refreshing drink in the Caribbean.

Ice cubes (optional)

1 **lime quarter**

4 oz (½ cup) **lager**

4 oz (½ cup) **ginger beer**

Half fill glass with ice (if using). Squeeze lime over top, twisting rind to release oils.

Add lager and ginger beer, stirring to combine.

Change It Up

CLASSIC SHANDY

Substitute lemon-lime soda (such as 7Up or Sprite) for the ginger beer.

207

Makes 1 serving. PER SERVING: about 177 cal, 1 g pro, trace total fat (0 g sat. fat), 37 g carb, 0 g fibre, 0 mg chol, 10 mg sodium. % RDI: 1% calcium, 1% iron, 5% vit C, 6% folate.

Macuá

This national drink of Nicaragua is named after the macaw, a colourful Central American bird. Light and fruity, the drink is garnished with a green cherry (to evoke the country's lush green landscapes) and an orange slice.

Ice cubes

1½ oz (3 tbsp) **aged rum** (such as Flor de Caña five-year-old Nicaraguan rum)

1 oz (2 tbsp) **guava juice** or guava nectar (such as Rubicon or Jumex)

1 oz (2 tbsp) **orange juice**

1 tbsp **lemon juice**

2 tsp **Simple Syrup** (page 203)

Orange slice

Green maraschino cherry

Fill cocktail shaker three-quarters full of ice. Pour in rum, guava juice, orange juice, lemon juice and simple syrup; shake well for 20 to 30 seconds.

Strain over ice in Tom Collins glass. Garnish with orange and cherry.

208

Change It Up

MACUÁ PITCHER

In pitcher, stir together 1½ cups aged rum, 1 cup each orange and guava juice, ½ cup lemon juice and ¼ cup Simple Syrup (page 203). Top with ice; stir until well chilled. Garnish with lemon and orange slices. **Makes 8 servings.**

VIRGIN MACUÁ

In ice-filled glass, combine 2 oz (¼ cup) each guava juice and orange juice and 1 oz (2 tbsp) lemon juice. Top with sparkling water. Garnish as directed. **Makes 1 serving.**

VIRGIN MACUÁ PITCHER

In pitcher, stir together 3 cups each orange juice and guava juice, and ½ cup lemon juice. Top with 1½ cups sparkling water and ice; stir until well chilled. Garnish with lemon and orange slices. **Makes 10 to 12 servings.**

Makes 1 serving. PER SERVING: about 159 cal, trace pro, trace total fat (0 g sat. fat), 17 g carb, trace fibre, 0 mg chol, 6 mg sodium, 84 mg potassium. % RDI: 1% calcium, 1% iron, 1% vit A, 35 vit C, 7% folate.

Rum Punch for One

This recipe is based on the classic Caribbean punch formula of 1 part sour (lime juice), 2 parts sweet (guava juice), 3 parts strong (rum) and 4 parts weak (coconut water). It's a refreshing summer drink.

1 tbsp **lime juice**

1 oz (2 tbsp) **guava juice,** pineapple juice or mango juice

1½ oz (3 tbsp) **amber rum**

2 oz (¼ cup) **coconut water** or soursop juice

Ice cubes

In Tom Collins glass, stir together lime juice, guava juice, rum and coconut water. Top with ice.

Dress It Up

COCONUT CUP

If you can get your hands on a young, fresh coconut, use the water inside to mix the cocktail, then serve it right in the coconut shell.

210

Makes 1 serving. PER SERVING: about 220 cal, 1 g pro, 12 g total fat (10 g sat. fat), 7 g carb, 1 g fibre, 0 mg chol, 8 mg sodium. % RDI: 2% calcium, 14% iron, 20% vit C, 7% folate.

Tropical Tutti-Frutti Punch

This refreshing fruit-and-cream concoction makes a great centrepiece for a children's party or a tropical-themed backyard barbecue.

1½ cups **pineapple juice**

2 cans (each 355 mL) **coconut milk**

1 cup **mango juice**

1 cup **passion fruit juice**

⅓ cup **lime juice**

3 cups **lemon-lime soda** (such as 7Up or Sprite)

4 cups **ice cubes**

In punch bowl, stir together pineapple juice, coconut milk, mango juice, passion fruit juice and lime juice.

Stir in lemon-lime soda; stir in ice cubes.

How-To

MAKING AN ICE RING

An ice ring is the best way to keep punch cool – it melts more slowly than ice cubes, so it won't dilute the punch as much. To make one, fill a Bundt pan or gelatin mould with cold water. (If you don't have one, a halved clean milk carton makes a great ice block.) Freeze until solid, about 8 hours. That's it! An ice ring is even prettier with whole berries or citrus slices suspended in it. To begin, add enough cold water to mould to come 1 inch (2.5 cm) up side; freeze until solid, about 1 hour. Add berries or citrus slices and enough cold water to just cover; freeze until solid, about 30 minutes. Fill with cold water and freeze until solid, about 8 hours. Just before serving, place ice ring mould in a warm water bath for about 30 seconds to loosen. Float on punch.

211

Makes **24 servings.** PER SERVING: about 90 cal, 1 g pro, 6 g total fat (5 g sat. fat), 9 g carb, trace fibre, 0 mg chol, 9 mg sodium, 120 mg potassium. % RDI: 1% calcium, 7% iron, 4% vit A, 12% vit C, 4% folate.

Mojito Punch

With the perfect tension between sweet and tart, this punch is a pretty option for a shower or a summertime party. Save the tips of the mint stems to sprinkle into the punch bowl as a garnish.

2 cups **fresh mint leaves**

2 cans (each 250 mL) **frozen Bacardi Mixers Margarita mix**

3½ cups **soda water**

1 bottle (750 mL) **white rum**

3 **limes,** sliced

3 cups **ice cubes**

In blender, purée together mint leaves, margarita mix and 1 cup water. Strain through cheesecloth-lined sieve into punch bowl.

Stir in soda water, rum, lime slices and ice cubes.

213

Makes 24 servings. PER SERVING: about 135 cal, trace pro, trace total fat (0 g sat. fat), 18 g carb, 0 g fibre, 0 mg chol, 10 mg sodium, 42 mg potassium. % RDI: 2% calcium, 6% iron, 3% vit A, 12% vit C, 4% folate.

Ginger Rhubarb Punch

Pretty, pink and slightly spicy from the fresh ginger, this lovely virgin punch is perfect for a crowd that doesn't want a spiked beverage.

1 cup sliced **fresh ginger**

4 cups **frozen chopped rhubarb**

¾ cup **granulated sugar**

2 cups **ginger ale**

¼ cup **lemon juice**

3 cups **ice cubes**

In large saucepan, cover and bring ginger and 4 cups water to boil. Add rhubarb and sugar; reduce heat and simmer until sugar is dissolved, about 10 minutes.

Strain rhubarb mixture into heatproof punch bowl or pitcher; let cool completely. Cover and refrigerate for 1 hour.

Stir in ginger ale and lemon juice. Stir in ice cubes.

214

Makes 12 servings. PER SERVING: about 71 cal, trace pro, trace total fat (0 g sat. fat), 18 g carb, 0 g fibre, 0 mg chol, 5 mg sodium, 55 mg potassium. % RDI: 8% calcium, 1% iron, 5% vit C, 1% folate.

Mulled Cranberry Tea

There's nothing like a warm drink to welcome guests on a cold winter day. Sweeten this tea with honey or sugar, if desired.

4 **cinnamon sticks,** broken

2 **whole star anise**

6 **whole cloves**

2 strips (each 3 x 1 inch/
   8 x 2.5 cm) **orange zest**

4 cups **cranberry cocktail**

4 cups hot **brewed tea**

Tie cinnamon sticks, star anise, cloves and orange zest in cheesecloth square.

In saucepan, heat cranberry cocktail with spice bag over low heat for 15 minutes.

Discard spice bag; stir in tea. Keep warm.

Change It Up

*MULLED
CRANBERRY WINE*
Substitute red wine for tea.

215

Makes 8 servings. PER SERVING: about 37 cal, 0 g pro, 0 g total fat (0 g sat. fat), 9 g carb, 0 g fibre, 0 mg chol, 3 mg sodium. % RDI: 37% vit C, 1% folate.

Frosty Peach Daiquiris

Peaches give this daiquiri a smooth texture and a heavenly flavour. If you're short on time, use frozen sliced peaches. They'll make the drink extra frosty.

3 cups **ice cubes**

3 cups sliced peeled **peaches**

¾ cup **white rum** or amber rum

6 tbsp **peach schnapps**

6 tbsp **lime juice**

⅓ cup **instant dissolving (fruit/berry) sugar** or icing sugar

In blender, pulse together ice, peaches, rum, peach schnapps, lime juice and sugar until ice is crushed.

Blend on high until smooth and slushy. Pour into pitcher.

216

How-To

PEELING PEACHES

With sharp knife, score X into bottom of each peach. In saucepan of boiling water, blanch peaches, a few at a time, until skins start to peel, 30 seconds. Submerge immediately in ice water; let cool enough to handle. Peel off skins.

Makes 6 servings. PER SERVING: about 201 cal, 1 g pro, trace total fat (0 g sat. fat), 29 g carb, 1 g fibre, 0 mg chol, 5 mg sodium. % RDI: 1% calcium, 2% iron, 3% vit A, 12% vit C, 2% folate.

Lime Squash

Cool and refreshing, this nonalcoholic beverage looks great in a pitcher with ice cubes – and tastes even better.

1¼ cups **lime juice** (about 6 limes)

⅓ cup **liquid honey**

Ice cubes

2 bottles (750 mL each)
   soda water

In heatproof glass measure, microwave lime juice with honey on high for 30 seconds; whisk until honey is dissolved. Let cool.

Fill pitcher half full of ice. Pour in soda water; stir in lime mixture.

Change It Up

HARD LIME SQUASH
For a spiked punch, stir in 1½ cups vodka along with lime mixture.

218

Makes 8 servings. PER SERVING: about 53 cal, trace pro, 0 g total fat (0 g sat. fat), 15 g carb, 0 g fibre, 0 mg chol, 3 mg sodium. % RDI: 3% calcium, 1% iron, 20% vit C, 2% folate.

Lemon Gin Fizz

Choose a gin with a light citrus accent, such as Hendrick or Plymouth, for this bubbly cocktail.

Ice cubes

1½ oz (3 tbsp) **gin**

1 oz (2 tbsp) **lemon juice** (about half lemon)

1½ tsp **instant dissolving (fruit/berry) sugar** or superfine sugar

2 oz (¼ cup) **soda water**

Lemon twist (see How-To, page 200)

Fill cocktail shaker with ice. Add gin, lemon juice and sugar; shake vigorously to blend and chill.

Strain into martini glass; top with soda water. Garnish with lemon twist.

219

Change It Up

MEYER LEMON GIN FIZZ

When they're in season, squeeze Meyer lemons to make the lemon juice. A cross between mandarins and lemons, Meyers have a sweet edge that complements their pleasing acidity.

Makes 1 serving. PER SERVING: about 113 cal, trace pro, 0 g total fat (0 g sat. fat), 9 g carb, 0 g fibre, 0 mg chol, 13 mg sodium. % RDI: 22% vit C, 2% folate.

From left: Lemon
Gin Fizz (page 219)
and Watermelon
Lemonade (opposite)

Watermelon Lemonade

Get the party started with a refreshing drink that features one of the favourite fruits of summer. There are plenty of versions to suit all kinds of palates.

1 cup **boiling water**

⅓ cup **granulated sugar**

5 cups cubed seeded **watermelon**

¾ cup **lemon juice**

In glass measure, whisk boiling water with sugar until dissolved. Set aside.

In blender, blend watermelon with lemon juice until smooth. Strain into pitcher, pressing mixture to extract liquid; stir in sugar syrup. *(Make-ahead: Cover and refrigerate for up to 1 week.)*

Change It Up

HARD WATERMELON LEMONADE

Fill highball glass with ice. Add ½ cup Watermelon Lemonade and 1 oz (2 tbsp) vodka; stir to combine. **Makes 1 serving.**

SPARKLING WATERMELON LEMONADE

Fill highball glass with ice. Add ¾ cup Watermelon Lemonade. Top with 1 tbsp soda water; stir to combine. **Makes 1 serving.**

SLUSHY VODKA WATERMELON LEMONADE

Omit boiling water. Decrease watermelon to 4 cups and freeze until firm. Increase sugar to ½ cup. In glass measure, microwave lemon juice with sugar at high for 1 minute. Whisk until sugar is dissolved. In blender, blend together half of the watermelon, 2 cups ice cubes, ½ cup vodka and half of the lemon syrup until smooth; pour into serving pitcher. Repeat once; stir to blend batches.

221

Makes 10 servings. PER SERVING: about 55 cal, 1 g pro, trace total fat (0 g sat. fat), 14 g carb, trace fibre, 0 mg chol, 6 mg sodium. % RDI: 1% calcium, 1% iron, 3% vit A, 20% vit C, 2% folate.

Pomegranate Martini Pitcher

You can serve this trendy cocktail without the hassle of shaking each one individually. Have soda water handy for guests to add their own splash. Be sure to use 100 per cent pomegranate juice for best flavour.

2⅔ cups **vodka**

2⅔ cups **pomegranate juice**

6 tbsp **orange-flavoured liqueur**

Ice cubes

GARNISH:

12 **fresh blueberries**

12 **orange wedges**

12 **fresh cranberries**

GARNISH: Thread 1 each blueberry, orange wedge and cranberry onto each of 12 skewers. Place in decorative glass, ready to add to each serving. *(Make-ahead: Cover and refrigerate for up to 12 hours.)*

In 6-cup (1.5 L) pitcher, stir together vodka, pomegranate juice and orange-flavoured liqueur; top with ice. Stir to blend and chill.

To serve, pour into glasses; garnish with skewers.

222

Makes 12 servings. PER SERVING: about 187 cal, trace pro, 0 g total fat (0 g sat. fat), 14 g carb, trace fibre, 0 mg chol, 6 mg sodium. % RDI: 1% calcium, 12% vit C, 1% folate.

Pitcher Cosmopolitans

Cosmos have a fresh, fruity flavour that's delicious as an appetite whetter before dinner. This pitcher version is terrific for parties.

1½ cups **vodka**

½ cup **cranberry juice**

¼ cup **orange-flavoured liqueur**

2 tbsp **lime juice**

Ice cubes

8 **frozen cranberries** (optional)

8 **lime slices**

In pitcher, stir together vodka, cranberry juice, orange-flavoured liqueur and lime juice. Top with ice; stir until well chilled.

Garnish each of 8 glasses with cranberry (if using) and lime slice. Strain cocktail into glasses.

Change It Up

VIRGIN PITCHER COSMOPOLITANS

Omit vodka and orange-flavoured liqueur. Increase cranberry juice to 2 cups. Add 1 cup ginger ale, ½ cup orange juice and 2 tbsp lime juice. Top with ice.

223

Makes 8 servings. PER SERVING: about 139 cal, trace pro, 0 g total fat (0 g sat. fat), 7 g carb, trace fibre, 0 mg chol, 1 mg sodium. % RDI: 1% iron, 8% vit C.

Classic Lemonade

Tart and tangy, unlike commercial lemonade, this is a back-porch essential. For a sparkling version, use soda water instead of plain water.

8 **lemons**

1 cup **granulated sugar**

3 cups **boiling water**

2 cups **ice cubes**

Lemon slices

Scrub lemons; rinse and dry. In large heatproof bowl and working with 1 lemon at a time, rub vigorously with about one-third of the sugar. Brush sugar off lemons and back into bowl.

Halve and squeeze lemons to make about 1½ cups juice; pour juice over sugar in bowl. Add remaining sugar and squeezed lemon shells.

Cover with boiling water, stirring until sugar is dissolved; let cool. Strain through cheesecloth-lined sieve, pressing out liquid. Let syrup cool. *(Make-ahead: Refrigerate in airtight container for up to 1 week.)*

In serving pitcher, combine syrup with 2 cups water; stir in ice to chill. Garnish with lemon slices.

224

Makes 8 to 10 servings. PER EACH OF 10 SERVINGS: about 87 cal, trace pro, 0 g total fat (0 g sat. fat), 23 g carb, trace fibre, 0 mg chol, 3 mg sodium. % RDI: 1% calcium, 27% vit C, 2% folate.

Sparkling Raspberry Lemonade

Tart-sweet and refreshingly fizzy, this pink lemonade is even better when garnished with mint and raspberries.

2½ cups **raspberries** (fresh or thawed frozen)

1½ cups **lemon juice** (about 8 lemons)

¾ cup **granulated sugar**

2¾ cups **soda water**

4 cups **ice cubes**

In large saucepan, bring raspberries, lemon juice and sugar to boil. Reduce heat to medium-low; simmer, mashing fruit, until sugar is dissolved, about 3 minutes.

Strain raspberry mixture through cheesecloth-lined sieve, pressing out liquid. Let syrup cool. *(Make-ahead: Refrigerate in airtight container for up to 1 week.)*

In serving pitcher, combine raspberry syrup with soda water; stir in ice to chill.

226

Makes 8 to 10 servings. PER EACH OF 10 SERVINGS: about 78 cal, trace pro, trace total fat (0 g sat. fat), 20 g carb, 0 g fibre, 0 mg chol, 17 mg sodium. % RDI: 1% calcium, 1% iron, 37% vit C, 4% folate.

Best Caesar

You'll be surprised at how much tastier one of Canada's best-loved drinks is when it's mixed with this homemade juice blend. Bottled clam juice is available at most supermarkets.

1 bottle (240 mL) **clam juice**

4½ cups **tomato juice** or vegetable cocktail

1 cup **vodka**

2 tbsp **lime juice**

1 tbsp **prepared horseradish**

1 tbsp **Worcestershire sauce**

½ tsp **hot pepper sauce**

¼ tsp **pepper**

Ice cubes

GARNISHES:

Celery salt

8 **lime slices**

Small celery stalks

In pitcher, stir together clam and tomato juices, vodka, lime juice, horseradish, Worcestershire sauce, hot pepper sauce and pepper; top with ice. Stir to chill.

GARNISHES: Rim glasses with celery salt (see How-To, below); pour in tomato juice mixture. Garnish with lime slices and celery.

227

How-To

RIMMING A GLASS

Whether you want a sweet, salty or spicy coating on a glass, you need to start with a citrus wedge. For this Caesar, sprinkle celery salt on a flat plate, then rub a lime wedge along the rim of the glass to moisten; dip the rim into the celery salt. The same process applies for a salt-rimmed glass (for a margarita) or a sugar-rimmed glass (for a special sweet martini).

Makes 8 servings. PER SERVING (WITHOUT GARNISHES): about 92 cal, 1 g pro, trace total fat (0 g sat. fat), 7 g carb, 1 g fibre, 1 mg chol, 575 mg sodium, 371 mg potassium. % RDI: 2% calcium, 7% iron, 8% vit A, 23% vit C, 13% folate.

From left: Kiwi
Margarita and
Strawberry Margarita

Classic Margarita

Make this pitcher-size perennial favourite with white or gold tequila, as desired. The better the tequila, the better the final result.

1½ cups **tequila**

½ cup **clear orange-flavoured liqueur** (such as Cointreau or Triple Sec)

⅓ cup **lime juice**

Ice cubes

GARNISHES:

Coarse salt

Lime wedges

In pitcher, stir together tequila, orange-flavoured liqueur and lime juice. Top with ice; stir well to blend and chill.

GARNISHES: Rim glasses with coarse salt (see How-To, page 227); strain margarita mixture into glasses. Garnish with lime wedges.

229

Change It Up

STRAWBERRY MARGARITA

Stir in 1 cup puréed frozen strawberries. Garnish each glass with 1 fresh strawberry.

KIWI MARGARITA

Stir in 1 cup puréed peeled cored kiwifruits (about 8). Garnish each glass with 1 slice kiwifruit and 1 fresh strawberry.

Makes 8 servings. PER SERVING (WITHOUT GARNISHES): about 162 cal, 0 g pro, trace total fat (0 g sat. fat), 8 g carb, 0 g fibre, 0 mg chol, 1 mg sodium, 13 mg potassium. % RDI: 5% vit C.

Hot Rum-Spiced Cider

Nothing warms up a cold night like a cup of rum-spiked mulled cider. Keep this punch warm in a slow cooker or on the stove top.

8 cups **sweetened apple cider**

2 cups **spiced rum**

6 **whole cloves**

4 each **star anise** and **green cardamom pods**

1 **cinnamon stick**

1 strip (2 inches/5 cm) **lemon zest**

GARNISH:

1 **apple,** sliced

2 tbsp **lemon juice**

In saucepan over medium-high heat, bring cider, rum, cloves, star anise, cardamom, cinnamon stick, lemon zest and 2 cups water just to simmer. Reduce heat to low; cook, without simmering, for 10 minutes.

GARNISH: Toss apple with lemon juice; stir into punch.

230

Change It Up

HOT RUM-SPICED APPLE CRANBERRY CIDER

Substitute apple cranberry cider for the apple cider. Garnish with ⅓ cup fresh cranberries.

Makes 12 servings. PER SERVING: about 124 cal, trace pro, 0 g total fat (0 g sat. fat), 25 g carb, trace fibre, 0 mg chol, 7 mg sodium, 213 mg potassium. % RDI: 1% calcium, 6% iron, 3% vit C.

Honey Apple Snack Mix

A little sweet and a little salty, this party mix is a hit with cocktails. Try it with walnuts or almonds instead of the peanuts and pecans if you prefer.

4 cups **woven wheat cereal squares** (such as Shreddies)

3 **rice cakes,** broken in small pieces

1 cup **pretzel sticks**

½ cup each **unsalted roasted peanuts** and **pecan pieces**

2 tbsp packed **brown sugar**

2½ tsp **garlic powder**

1¼ tsp **chili powder**

Pinch **salt**

⅓ cup **unsweetened applesauce**

3 tbsp **butter**

2 tbsp **liquid honey**

In bowl, combine cereal squares, rice cakes, pretzels, peanuts, pecans, brown sugar, garlic powder, chili powder and salt.

In small saucepan, heat applesauce, butter and honey over medium-low heat until butter is melted, about 2 minutes. Stir into cereal mixture, tossing to coat. Spread on rimmed baking sheet.

Bake in 325°F (160°C) oven, stirring occasionally, until cereal squares are deep golden, 18 to 20 minutes. Let cool. *(Make-ahead: Store in airtight container for up to 5 days.)*

232

Makes 8 cups. PER ¼ CUP: about 76 cal, 2 g pro, 4 g total fat (1 g sat. fat), 10 g carb, 1 g fibre, 3 mg chol, 77 mg sodium, 58 mg potassium. % RDI: 1% calcium, 8% iron, 1% vit A, 4% folate.

Curried Nuts & Bolts

This updated party mix is a little healthier than the original 1960s version, and it gets a more exotic edge from the mix of curry spices.

2 cups **small pretzels**

1½ cups **multigrain cereal circles** (such as Cheerios)

1½ cups **woven wheat cereal squares** (such as Shreddies)

1½ cups **mini cheese crackers**

1 cup **whole blanched almonds**

⅓ cup **butter**

1 tbsp **mild curry paste** or curry powder

¼ tsp **garlic powder**

In large bowl, combine pretzels, cereal circles, cereal squares, cheese crackers and almonds.

In small saucepan, melt together butter, curry paste and garlic powder. Pour over pretzel mixture, tossing to coat. Spread on rimmed baking sheet.

Bake in 350°F (180°C) oven, stirring twice, until golden, 20 to 25 minutes. *(Make-ahead: Store in airtight container for up to 1 week.)*

234

Makes about 7 cups. PER ¼ CUP: about 95 cal, 2 g pro, 6 g total fat (2 g sat. fat), 9 g carb, 1 g fibre, 8 mg chol, 146 mg sodium. % RDI: 3% calcium, 8% iron, 3% vit A, 3% folate.

Masala Snack Mix

Look for roasted soybeans and sesame sticks in your grocery store's bulk aisle or at the local bulk food store.

1 can (19 oz/540 mL) **chickpeas,** drained and rinsed

¾ cup **sesame sticks**

½ cup **unsalted roasted cashews**

½ cup **unsalted roasted soybeans**

¼ cup **unsalted hulled raw pumpkin seeds**

2 tbsp **vegetable oil**

1 tbsp **mild curry paste**

2 tsp **lime juice**

1 tsp **garam masala**

Pinch **salt**

On foil-lined rimmed baking sheet, toast chickpeas in 400°F (200°C) oven, stirring once, until golden and crunchy, about 30 minutes. Let cool on pan on rack for 5 minutes.

Meanwhile, in large bowl, combine sesame sticks, cashews, soybeans and pumpkin seeds. Add chickpeas; toss to combine.

Whisk together oil, curry paste, lime juice, garam masala and salt; add to chickpea mixture and toss to coat. Roast on same baking sheet in 350°F (180°C) oven until fragrant and golden, about 12 minutes. *(Make-ahead: Store in airtight container for up to 2 weeks.)*

235

Makes about 3 cups. PER ¼ CUP: about 172 cal, 8 g pro, 12 g total fat (1 g sat. fat), 16 g carb, 4 g fibre, 0 mg chol, 204 mg sodium. % RDI: 4% calcium, 12% iron, 20% folate.

Asian Party Mix

Roasted peanuts with just a hint of hot Japanese horseradish are the base for this crunchy snack. Look for tubes of prepared wasabi paste in the supermarket deli, usually near the sushi display.

2 tbsp **butter,** softened

⅔ cup **granulated sugar**

3 cups **unsalted roasted peanuts**

2 tbsp **wasabi paste**

2 tsp **coarse sea salt**

1 cup **wasabi peas**

1 cup **mixed mini Asian rice crackers** or bean crackers

Line large rimmed baking sheet with foil or parchment paper; with fingers, spread with butter. Set aside.

In saucepan, bring sugar and ⅔ cup water to boil, stirring to dissolve sugar; boil for 5 minutes. Remove from heat. Stir in peanuts; let stand for 5 minutes, stirring often.

Drain peanuts in sieve and return to saucepan; stir in wasabi paste and salt. Spread on prepared pan; roast in 350°F (180°C) oven, stirring once, until golden, about 15 minutes. Let cool on pan on rack, stirring occasionally.

Toss together nuts, wasabi peas and crackers. *(Make-ahead: Store in airtight container for up to 2 weeks.)*

237

Makes about 5 cups. PER ¼ CUP: about 193 cal, 7 g pro, 13 g total fat (2 g sat. fat), 12 g carb, 2 g fibre, 4 mg chol, 203 mg sodium. % RDI: 2% calcium, 4% iron, 1% vit A, 12% folate.

Curried Roasted Chickpeas

This flavourful snack is low in saturated fat and a source of iron and folate. But it's so delicious you won't stop to think about how healthy it is.

2 tbsp **olive oil**

2 tsp **curry powder**

¼ tsp **garlic powder**

¼ tsp **ground cumin**

¼ tsp **ground coriander**

¼ tsp **salt**

1 can (19 oz/540 mL) **chickpeas**

In large bowl, stir together oil, curry powder, garlic powder, cumin, coriander and salt.

Drain and rinse chickpeas; pat dry with towel. Add to bowl, stirring to coat. Spread on rimmed baking sheet.

Bake in 400°F (200°C) oven, stirring occasionally, until golden, crisp and dried, 35 to 38 minutes.

238

Makes 1⅓ cups. PER ¼ CUP: about 150 cal, 4 g pro, 6 g total fat (trace sat. fat), 20 g carb, 4 g fibre, 0 mg chol, 326 mg sodium, 142 mg potassium. % RDI: 2% calcium, 10% iron, 4% vit C, 22% folate.

Maple Chili Snack Mix

Ho-hum whole wheat cereal gets jazzed up in this energy-packed sweet and savoury mix that's delicious with beer.

5 cups **small whole wheat cereal squares** (such as Spoon Size Shredded Wheat)

1 cup **raisins**

½ cup each chopped **dried pears** and chopped **dried apricots**

½ cup each **slivered almonds** and **unsalted roasted peanuts**

⅓ cup **butter**

⅓ cup **maple syrup**

1 tbsp **chili powder**

¼ tsp **salt**

Dash **hot pepper sauce**

In large bowl, toss together cereal squares, raisins, pears, apricots, almonds and peanuts; set aside.

In small saucepan, bring butter, maple syrup, chili powder, salt and hot pepper sauce to boil over medium heat; boil for 1 minute. Pour over cereal mixture, tossing to coat. Spread on rimmed baking sheet.

Bake in 325°F (160°C) oven, stirring occasionally, until lightly toasted, 10 to 12 minutes. Let cool on pan on rack. *(Make-ahead: Store in airtight container for up to 1 week.)*

239

Makes 8 cups. PER ¼ CUP: about 105 cal, 2 g pro, 4 g total fat (2 g sat. fat), 17 g carb, 3 g fibre, 5 mg chol, 36 mg sodium, 156 mg potassium. % RDI: 2% calcium, 7% iron, 3% vit A, 1% vit C, 4% folate.

Barbecue Roasted Almonds

If you're a fan of barbecue-flavour chips, these spicy-sweet almonds are just the ticket for your next party. You might want to make a double batch since they disappear so quickly. Sprinkle any leftovers over salad.

2½ cups **whole blanched almonds**

2 tbsp **fancy molasses**

1 tbsp packed **brown sugar**

1 tbsp **chili powder**

1 tbsp **vegetable oil**

1½ tsp **cider vinegar**

½ tsp each **ground cumin** and **salt**

¼ tsp **garlic powder**

Pinch **cayenne pepper**

On parchment paper–lined baking sheet, toast almonds in 350°F (180°C) oven until fragrant but not browned, about 7 minutes.

Meanwhile, whisk together molasses, brown sugar, chili powder, oil, vinegar, cumin, salt, garlic powder and cayenne pepper; drizzle over almonds, tossing to coat. Bake, stirring halfway through, for 8 minutes.

Turn off oven; leave nuts in oven for 8 minutes. Let cool on pan on rack until crisp and dry; break clusters apart. (*Make-ahead: Store in airtight container for up to 2 weeks. If softening, crisp in 350°F/180°C oven for about 5 minutes.*)

240

Makes about 3 cups. PER 1 TBSP: about 50 cal, 2 g pro, 4 g total fat (trace sat. fat), 3 g carb, 1 g fibre, 0 mg chol, 28 mg sodium. % RDI: 2% calcium, 3% iron, 1% vit A, 1% folate.

From left: Mustard-
Spiced Nuts (page 244)
and Barbecue Roasted
Almonds (opposite)

Candied Walnuts

Sweet, with just a touch of spice from the cayenne, these walnuts are the perfect nibble for nut lovers who have a sweet tooth.

⅓ cup **corn syrup**

2 tbsp **granulated sugar**

1 tsp **salt**

Pinch each **cinnamon** and **cayenne pepper**

2½ cups **walnut halves** (about 8 oz/225 g)

In bowl, combine corn syrup, sugar, salt, cinnamon and cayenne pepper; stir in walnuts until coated. Spread on well-greased rimmed baking sheet.

Bake in 325°F (160°C) oven, stirring occasionally to break up clumps, until bubbling and nuts are deep golden, about 15 minutes. Let cool on pan on rack. *(Make-ahead: Store in airtight container for up to 3 days.)*

242

Makes 2½ cups. PER 1 TBSP: about 51 cal, 1 g pro, 4 g total fat (trace sat. fat), 4 g carb, trace fibre, 0 mg chol, 61 mg sodium. % RDI: 1% calcium, 1% iron, 3% folate.

Tamari Almonds

These irresistible nibbles won't stick around for long. Tamari is similar to soy sauce, with a slightly more mellow flavour. It's often wheat-free, so these can be a delicious gluten-free treat – just check the label to be sure.

2½ cups **whole unblanched almonds**

¼ cup **tamari** or soy sauce

1 tsp **lemon juice**

Pinch **cayenne pepper** (optional)

On parchment paper–lined rimmed baking sheet, toast almonds in 350°F (180°C) oven until fragrant, about 5 minutes.

Sprinkle nuts with tamari, lemon juice, and cayenne pepper (if using); toss to coat. Bake for 7 minutes.

Stir nuts and turn off oven; leave nuts in oven until tamari mixture is absorbed, 10 to 12 minutes. Let cool on pan on rack until crisp and dry. *(Make-ahead: Store in airtight container for up to 2 weeks. If softening, crisp in 350°F/180°C oven for about 5 minutes.)*

243

Makes 2½ cups. PER 1 TBSP: about 53 cal, 2 g pro, 5 g total fat (1 g sat. fat), 2 g carb, 1 g fibre, 0 mg chol, 90 mg sodium. % RDI: 2% calcium, 3% iron, 2% folate.

Mustard-Spiced Nuts

This quick mix is irresistible, and you can whip it up at the last minute. The seasonings will work with any mix of unsalted nuts you have on hand.

1 cup **walnut halves**

1 cup **natural almonds**

1 cup **raw cashews**

1 cup shelled **pistachios**

1 tbsp **extra-virgin olive oil**

1 tbsp **Dijon mustard**

2 tbsp packed **brown sugar**

1 tbsp **dry mustard**

1½ tsp **ground coriander**

1 tsp **salt**

½ tsp **cayenne pepper**

¼ tsp **pepper**

In bowl, stir together walnuts, almonds, cashews, pistachios, oil and Dijon mustard until coated. Combine brown sugar, dry mustard, coriander, salt, and cayenne and black peppers; toss with nuts to coat.

Bake on parchment paper–lined baking sheet in 300°F (150°C) oven, stirring once, until fragrant and lightly toasted, about 20 minutes. *(Make-ahead: Store in airtight container for up to 1 week.)*

244

Makes 4 cups. PER 1 TBSP: about 51 cal, 2 g pro, 4 g total fat (1 g sat. fat), 3 g carb, 1 g fibre, 0 mg chol, 40 mg sodium, 60 mg potassium. % RDI: 1% calcium, 3% iron, 2% folate.

Gingered Pecans

Perfect for partytime munching, these zippy pecans can add crunch to a sundae and are wonderful in a fruit crisp or mixed green salad.

2½ cups **pecan halves**

3 tbsp **granulated sugar**

1½ tsp **coarse sea salt**

½ tsp **ground ginger**

1 tbsp **apricot jam**

1½ tsp **vegetable oil**

On rimmed baking sheet, toast pecans in 350°F (180°C) oven, stirring occasionally, until fragrant, about 10 minutes.

Meanwhile, in large bowl, combine sugar, salt and ginger; set aside.

In small saucepan, bring ¼ cup water, apricot jam and oil to boil; reduce heat to medium-low. Add pecans; stir to coat. Cook, stirring, until almost no liquid remains, about 3 minutes. Transfer to sugar mixture; toss until well coated.

Spread pecans on parchment paper–lined rimmed baking sheets; let cool. *(Make-ahead: Store in airtight container for up to 1 week.)*

245

Makes about 3 cups. PER 1 TBSP: about 45 cal, 1 g pro, 4 g total fat (trace sat. fat), 2 g carb, 1 g fibre, 0 mg chol, 72 mg sodium. % RDI: 1% calcium, 1% iron, 1% folate.

ACKNOWLEDGMENTS

APPETIZERS ARE THE PERFECT FOOD IN MY OPINION.

I love the variety of shapes, textures and flavours they offer. They're a little like the cast of characters it takes to put together each of *Canadian Living*'s many cookbooks: Some are sweet, some are salty, some are dynamic and some are just plain dependable. And all together, they make the party so much fun.

For their hard work on this project, I'd like to thank the following individuals:

246

- Food director Annabelle Waugh and her sensational team, The Canadian Living Test Kitchen, for creating and perfecting the tastiest appetizers on the planet – and for their trusted advice when it comes to planning the perfect party

- Art director Chris Bond for his vision, which has driven the look and feel of this very beautiful book from Day One

- Photographers Ryan Szulc and Edward Pond, food stylists Nicole Young and Claire Stubbs, and prop stylist Catherine Doherty for styling and photographing a mouthwatering array of delicious bites for this project

- Many more photographers and stylists for creating the other lovely photos in these pages (see page 256 for a complete list)

- Copy editor Julia Armstrong for making sure every page was spelled, punctuated and styled perfectly

- Beth Zabloski, our book indexer, for assembling an extensive, easy-to-navigate index that readers can really use

- Sharyn Joliat of Info Access for complete, accurate nutrient analysis

- Random House Canada for distribution and promotion of this book

- Transcontinental Books vice-president Marc Laberge, publishing director Mathieu de Lajartre and assistant editor Céline Comtois for smooth sailing from idea to finished book

- *Canadian Living* publisher Lynn Chambers and editor-in-chief Susan Antonacci for their tireless support of all of our endeavours – cookbook and otherwise

        – Tina Anson Mine, project editor

247

248

249

250

251

252

253

254

ABOUT OUR NUTRITION INFORMATION

To meet nutrient needs each day, moderately active women 25 to 49 need about 1,900 calories, 51 g protein, 261 g carbohydrate, 25 to 35 g fibre and not more than 63 g total fat (21 g saturated fat).

Men and teenagers usually need more. Canadian sodium intake of approximately 3,500 mg daily should be reduced, whereas the intake of potassium from food sources should be increased to 4,700 mg per day.

Percentage of recommended daily intake (% RDI) is based on the values used for Canadian food labels for calcium, iron, vitamins A and C, and folate.

Figures are rounded off. They are based on the first ingredient listed when there is a choice and do not include optional ingredients or those with no specified amounts.

ABBREVIATIONS

cal = calories
pro = protein
carb = carbohydrate
sat. fat = saturated fat
chol = cholesterol

255

TESTED TILL perfect

Our Tested-Till-Perfect guarantee means we've tested every recipe, using the same grocery store ingredients and household appliances as you do, until we're sure you'll get perfect results at home.

CREDITS

PHOTOGRAPHY

Ryan Brook/TC Media: back cover (portrait) and page 5 (portrait).

Jeff Coulson/TC Media: pages 5 (food), 11, 122 and 144.

Yvonne Duivenvoorden: pages 20, 25, 28, 41, 52, 72, 85, 88, 106, 111, 114, 119, 127, 153, 161, 171, 174, 180, 188, 209, 212, 228 and 231.

Joe Kim/TC Media: page 137.

Edward Pond: front cover; spine; pages 33, 36, 44, 49, 64, 69, 77, 80, 95, 156, 162, 185, 193, 201 and 225.

Jodi Pudge: page 12.

David Scott: pages 17, 140, 148 and 220.

Ryan Szulc: back cover (food); pages 7, 9, 15, 57, 61, 91, 93, 98, 103, 135, 167, 199, 204, 217, 233, 236 and 241.

Thinkstock: pages 10 and 13.

FOOD STYLING

Donna Bartolini: pages 28, 85 and 127.

Alison Kent: page 212.

Lucie Richard: pages 12, 17, 20, 33, 36, 41, 44, 49, 52, 72, 148, 185, 201 and 228.

Claire Stancer: pages 111, 171 and 174.

Claire Stubbs: front cover; spine; pages 5, 11, 64, 69, 77, 80, 88, 95, 106, 114, 119, 122, 137, 153, 156, 161, 162, 188, 193, 209, 225 and 231.

Rosemarie Superville: pages 25 and 140.

Sandra Watson: page 220.

Nicole Young: back cover; pages 7, 9, 15, 57, 61, 91, 93, 98, 103, 135, 144, 167, 199, 204, 217, 233, 236 and 241.

PROP STYLING

Laura Branson: pages 122 and 212.

Catherine Doherty: front and back covers; spine; pages 7, 9, 12, 15, 25, 33, 36, 41, 44, 49, 57, 61, 64, 69, 80, 91, 93, 95, 98, 103, 135, 144, 156, 167, 185, 193, 199, 201, 204, 217, 231, 233, 236 and 241.

Marc-Philippe Gagné: page 88.

Madeleine Johari: page 137.

Oksana Slavutych: pages 17, 20, 28, 52, 72, 77, 85, 106, 111, 114, 119, 127, 140, 148, 162, 171, 174, 180, 188, 220, 225 and 228.

Genevieve Wiseman: pages 5, 11, 153, 161 and 209.

256